ANSI C

Programming Guide

First Edition

Venkatesh Ramasamy

Lulu Press, Inc.
3101 Hillsborough Street
Raleigh, North Carolina, 27607
United States of America

ANSI C Programming Guide, First Edition

by Venkatesh Ramasamy

© Copyright 2013 Venkatesh Ramasamy. All rights reserved.

International Standard Book Number (ISBN): 978-1-304-62096-5

No part of this publication may be reproduced or distributed in any form or by any means, or stored in a database or retrieval system, without the prior written permission of the publisher, with the exception that the program listings may be entered, stored and executed in a computer system, but they may not be reproduced for publication.

Printed in the United States of America.

First Edition published on November 2013.

Disclaimer

No patent liability is assumed with respect to the use of the information contained herein. Although every precaution has been taken in the preparation of this book, the publisher and author assume no responsibility for errors or omissions. No liability is assumed for incidental or consequential damage in connection with or arising out of the use of the information or programs contained herein.

Printed and bounded in Lulu Press, Inc., 3101 Hillsborough Street, Raleigh, North Carolina, 27607, United States of America.

Preface

C is a general-purpose, procedural, imperative computer programming language developed in 1972 by Dennis M. Ritchie at the Bell Telephone Laboratories to develop the UNIX operating system. C is one of the widely used computer language and it keeps fluctuating at number one scale of popularity along with other programming language. C is currently the premier language for software developers as it's widely distributed and standard. The book **"ANSI C Programming Guide"** attempts to provide simple explanation for beginners about the various ANSI C programming concepts. This book is the single source you would need to quickly race up to speed and significantly enhance your skill and knowledge in ANSI C. This book has been designed as a self-study material for both beginners and experienced programmers.

This book is organized into five parts along with practical examples that will show you how to develop your program in ANSI C.

- **Part I - ANSI C Programming:** The first part is explained with 100 programming examples in ANSI C programming concepts which includes Operators, Expressions, Control Statements, Arrays, Strings, Structures, Union, Functions, Pointers, Files Handling, Memory Allocations, Preprocessors, etc.
- **Part II - ANSI C Syntax Rules:** The second part is explained with important syntax rules in ANSI C programming.

- **Part III - ANSI C Library Functions:** The third part is explained with library functions in ANSI C programming which includes Character functions, String functions, Mathematical functions, Dynamic Allocation functions, Utility functions, Input/Output functions, etc.
- **Part IV - ANSI C References:** The fourth part is explained with reference materials in ANSI C programming which includes Header Files, Type Conversion Characters, Keywords, Escape Sequences, Data Types, Preprocessors, etc.
- **Part V - ANSI C Aptitude Questions:** The fifth part is explained with aptitude and interview questions on ANSI C programming concepts with answers.

This book a perfect fit for all groups of people from beginners with no previous programming experience to programmers who already know C and are ambitious to improve their style and reliability. Whether coding in ANSI C is your hobby or your career, this book will enlighten you on your goal.

Happy Reading !!

About Programming Guide Series:

The titles in this programming guide series deals with technical descriptions of important software programming languages to give insights on how programming works and what it can be used for. These are ideal first books for beginners from a wide range of backgrounds like enterprise developer, technical manager, solution architect, tester, etc. This is an ideal place to begin mastering a new programming area and lay a solid foundation for further study. The curriculum of these books is carefully designed to reflect the needs of a diverse population, so there is something for everyone. The books in this programming guide series cover a broad range of topics including ANSI C, HTML, CSS, JavaScript, VBScript, JCL, VSAM, etc.

Warm Regards,
Venkatesh Ramasamy
twitter @rvenkateshbe

Author

Venkatesh Ramasamy is a senior quality engineer and technology consultant for a leading multinational company in Information Technology sector. He has excellent experience in managing enterprise IT project life cycle and has developed many software products for providing end-to-end IT services with optimized cost and improved quality. He is also vastly experienced in working with large insurers and financial services organizations based out of UK & US, for setting up independent test centers for their enterprise level quality engineering needs. He is very much interested in programming languages & web design technologies and has helped in developing wide variety of software products for the customers to successfully implement their new age corporate IT strategies.

Over the years he has presented and published many whitepapers at both national and international conferences and has also authored various technical articles in international magazines. He is also the author of several other programming books including ANSI C Programming Guide, HTML & CSS Programming Guide, JavaScript Programming Guide, JCL & VSAM Programming Guide and Handbook on 1000 Software Testing Tools.

You can reach him at his Twitter handle @rvenkateshbe.

Contents

Part: I - ANSI C Programming..............01

01. Program to perform multiplication and division operations
02. Program to calculate the area and perimeter of circle
03. Program to find the area of a triangle using three sides
04. Program to swap the given two numbers
05. Program to find the surface area and volume of cube using pow() method
06. Program to find whether given year is leap year or not
07. Program to find whether a given integer is odd or even
08. Program to check whether a given number is prime or not
09. Program to perform basic arithmetic operations using freehand operators
10. Program to calculate the average of ten numbers
11. Program to find the greatest of two number using conditional operator
12. Program to find the biggest of three numbers
13. Program to solve the given quadratic equation
14. Program to find the factorial of a given number
15. Program to swap the given two numbers using bitwise operator
16. Program (Magic Number Game) to illustrate the usage of rand() function
17. Program to illustrate the floor(), ceil(), fabs() functions

18. Program to convert the Fahrenheit temperature to Celsius
19. Program to find the quadrant of operation for the given co-ordinates
20. Program to convert the lower case character into upper case (vice versa)
21. Program to find whether a given character is alphanumeric
22. Program to perform basic arithmetic operations using switch statement
23. Program to fin the GCD and LCM of two integers
24. Program to generate Fibonacci numbers
25. Program to check whether the given number is palindrome or not
26. Program to accept an integer and find the sum of the digits in it
27. Program to perform the logical XNOR operation
28. Program to calculate the compound interest
29. Program to understand the usage of bitwise operator
30. Program to perform mark analysis using if else statement
31. Program to generate the prime numbers within the given limits
32. Program to search an element in an array
33. Program to calculate the median using arrays
34. Program to find the biggest of 10 numbers
35. Program to produce the multiplication table using for loop
36. Program to calculate the mean, variance and standard deviation
37. Program to find the largest number from 2 D array using functions
38. Program to find the factorial using recursion
39. Program to perform basic arithmetic operations using functions
40. Program to use nesting of functions
41. Program to read a line of text and reverse it using recursive function
42. Program to find the largest number using function
43. Program to produce Towers of Hanoi
44. Program to find the sum of series (1+2+3+....+N) using recursive function
45. Program to convert the given decimal number into binary number
46. Program to convert the given octal number into decimal number
47. Program to convert the given binary number into decimal number
48. Program to convert the given decimal number into octal number
49. Program to convert the given binary number into octal number
50. Program to perform Bubble Sort

51. Program to perform Selection Sort
52. Program to perform the Insertion Sort
53. Program to produce the following output:

    *
    **
    ***
    ****
    *****

54. Program to produce the following output:

    1
    22
    333
    4444
    55555

55. Program to produce the following output:

    1
    2 3
    4 5 6
    7 8 9 10

56. Program to produce the following output:

    *
    ***
    *****
    ****
    ****

57. Program to produce the following output:

    * $ $ $ $
    $ * $ $ $
    $ $ * $ $
    $ $ $ * $
    $ $ $ $ *

58. Program to produce the following output:

    # # # # #
    # # # # #
    # # 0 # #
    # # # # #
    # # # # #

59. Program to produce the following output:

    1
    234
    56789

60. Program to perform mark analysis using structures
61. Program to retrieve the mailing address using structures
62. Program to calculate the sum of all the elements in a matrix
63. Program to find whether the given is Diagonal Matrix or not
64. Program to find the given matrix is Unit Matrix
65. Program to extract the diagonal elements from the given matrix
66. Program to perform addition and subtraction of two matrix
67. Program to perform multiplication of two matrix
68. Program to interchange the main diagonal elements with that of the secondary diagonal elements
69. Program to find the transpose of given matrix
70. Program to extract the lower diagonal elements from the given matrix
71. Program to compare two strings
72. Program to concatenate two strings
73. Program to copy the strings and calculate the length of the string
74. Program to check the palindrome string
75. Program to concatenate two strings using strcat() function
76. Program to compare two strings using strcmp() function
77. Program to copy two strings using strcpy() function
78. Program to reverse the given string using strrev() function
79. Program to convert the case of the strings to upper case
80. Program to find sum of series (1+2+3+....+n)
81. Program to find the sum of series ($1^3+2^3+3^3+....+n^3$)

82. Program to calculate the sum of 1/n series
83. Program to find the sum of cos(x) series
84. Program to sort the given marks using pointers
85. Program to find largest number using pointers
86. Program to swap two numbers using pointers
87. Program to find the sum of squares of N numbers
88. Program to find length of the string using pointers
89. Program to count the number of vowels using pointers
90. Program to find the cube of a given number using macro definition
91. Program to find the area of circle using macro definition
92. Program to demonstrate the nesting of macros
93. Program to illustrate the usage of #ifdef, #ifndef
94. Program to illustrate the usage of Token Pasting Operator ##
95. Program to perform queue operations
96. Program to perform stack operations
97. Program to illustrate the dynamic memory allocation
98. Program to read and write characters in file
99. Program to separate positive and negative numbers using files
100. Program to calculate the total marks using files

Part: II - ANSI C Syntax Rules............105

Part: III - ANSI C Library Functions...125

01. Character Functions
02. String Functions
03. Mathematical Functions
04. Dynamic Allocation Functions
05. Utility Functions
06. Input / Output Functions

Part: IV - ANSI C References............131

01. Header Files
02. Type Conversion Character
03. Keywords
04. Escape Sequences
05. Data Types
06. Preprocessors

Part: V - ANSI C Aptitude Questions...137

Part - I

ANSI C PROGRAMMING

01. Program to perform multiplication and division operations

```c
/* Multiplication and Division */
#include<stdio.h>
#include<conio.h>
void main()
{
int a,b,c,d;
clrscr();
printf("Enter the values:\n");
scanf("%d %d",&a,&b);
c=a*b;
d=a/b;
printf("The multiplication value: %d\n",c);
printf("The division value: %d",d);
getch();
}

/*-----------------------------------------
Output:
Enter the values:
10 5
The multiplication value: 50
The division value: 2
-------------------------------------------*/
```

02. Program to calculate the area and perimeter of circle

```c
/* Area and perimeter of circle */
#include<stdio.h>
#include<conio.h>
#include<math.h>
#define PI 3.14
void main()
{
float r,area,perimeter;
clrscr();
printf("Enter the value of the Radius:\t");
```

```
scanf("%f",&r);
area=PI*r*r;
perimeter=2*PI*r;
printf("\nThe area of the circle: %f",area);
printf("\nThe perimeter of the circle: %f",perimeter);
getch();}
```

```
/*----------------------------------------
Output:
Enter the value of the Radius:  10.5
The area of the circle: 346.184998
The perimeter of the circle: 65.940002
--------------------------------------------*/
```

03. Program to find the area of a triangle using three sides

```c
/* Area of a triangle */
#include <stdio.h>
#include <conio.h>
#include <math.h>
void main()
{
int s, a, b, c, area;
clrscr();
printf("Enter the values of a,b and c\n");
scanf ("%d %d %d", &a, &b, &c);
s = (a + b + c) / 2;
area = sqrt ( s * (s-a) * (s-b) * (s-c));
printf ("Area of a triangle = %d\n", area);
getch();
}
```

```
/*-----------------------------
Output:
Enter the values of a,b and c
3 4 5
Area of a triangle = 6
-------------------------------*/
```

04. Program to swap the given two numbers

```c
/* Swapping */
#include<stdio.h>
#include<conio.h>
void main()
{
int a,b,t;
clrscr();
printf("Enter the values for a and b:\n");
scanf("%d %d",&a,&b);
printf("The value before swapping:a= %d b=%d\n",a,b);
t=b;
b=a;
a=t;
printf("The value after swapping:a= %d b=%d\n",a,b);
getch();
}

/*------------------------------------------
Output:
Enter the values for a and b:
5 10
The value before swapping:a=5 b=10
The value after swapping:a=10 b=5
----------------------------------------*/
```

05. Program to find the surface area and volume of cube using pow() method

```c
/* Surface area and Volume of cube */
#include <stdio.h>
#include<conio.h>
#include <math.h>
void main()
{
float  side, surfArea, volume;
clrscr();
```

```
printf("Enter the length of a side\n");
scanf("%f", &side);
surfArea = 6.0 * side * side;
volume = pow (side, 3);
printf("Surface area = %6.2f and Volume = %6.2f\n", surfArea, volume);
getch();
}
```

```
/*----------------------------------------------------
Output:
Enter the length of a side
4
Surface area =  96.00 and Volume =  64.00
-----------------------------------------------------*/
```

06. Program to find whether given year is leap year or not

```
/*Find leap year or not */
#include <stdio.h>
#include<conio.h>
void main()
{
int year;
clrscr();
printf("Enter a year\n");
scanf("%d",&year);
if ( (year % 4) == 0)
printf("%d is a leap year",year);
else
printf("%d is not a leap year\n",year);
getch();
}
```

```
/*----------------------------------------
Output:
Enter a year
2000
2000 is a leap year
```

Enter a year
2007
2007 is not a leap year
--*/

07. Program to find whether a given integer is odd or even

```c
/* Find odd or even*/
#include <stdio.h>
#include <conio.h>
void main()
{
int ival, remainder;
clrscr();
printf("Enter an integer :");
scanf ("%d", &ival);
remainder = ival % 2;
if (remainder == 0)
printf ("%d, is an even integer\n", ival);
else
printf ("%d, is an odd integer\n", ival);
getch();
}
```

/*---------------------------------
Output:
Enter an integer :13
13, is an odd integer

Enter an integer :24
24, is an even integer
------------------------------------*/

08. Program to check whether a given number is prime or not

```c
/* Find prime or not */
#include <stdio.h>
#include <stdlib.h>
```

```c
#include <conio.h>
void main()
{
int num, j, flag;
clrscr();
printf("Enter a number\n");
scanf("%d", &num);
if ( num <= 1)
{
printf("%d is not a prime numbers\n", num);
exit(1);
}
flag = 0;
for ( j=2; j<= num/2; j++)
{
if( ( num % j ) == 0)
{
flag = 1;
break;
}
}
if(flag == 0)
printf("%d is a prime number\n",num);
else
printf("%d is not a prime number\n", num);
getch();
}

/*----------------------------------------
Output:
Enter a number
34
34 is not a prime number
Enter a number
29
29 is a prime number
-------------------------------------------*/
```

09. Program to perform basic arithmetic operations using freehand operators

```c
/*Program to perform basic arithmetic operations using freehand operators*/
#include<stdio.h>
#include<conio.h>
void main()
{
 int a,b,c,d;
 clrscr();
 printf("Enter the values for a,b,c,d:\n");
 scanf("%d%d %d %d",&a,&b,&c,&d);
 a+=5;
 b-=5;
 c*=5;
 d/=5;
 printf("The new value of a,b,c,d:\t%d\t%d\t%d\t%d",a,b,c,d);
 getch();
}
```

```
/*----------------------------------------------------------
Output:
Enter the values for a,b,c,d:
10 20 30 40
The new value of a,b,c,d:      15    15    150    8
-----------------------------------------------------------*/
```

10. Program to calculate the average of ten numbers

```c
/*Program to calculate the average of ten numbers*/
#include<stdio.h>
#include<conio.h>
#define N 10
void main()
{
 int count;
  float sum,average,number;
```

```c
clrscr();
sum=0;
count=0;
printf("Enter the values:\n");
while(count<10)
{
scanf("%f",&number);
sum=sum+number;
count=count+1;
}
average=sum/N;
printf("The Sum= %f",sum);
printf("\nThe Average= %f",average);
getch();
}
```

```
/*-----------------------------------
Output:
Enter the values:
1 2 3 4 5 6 7 8 9 10
The Sum= 55.000000
The Average= 5.500000
---------------------------------------*/
```

11. Program to find the greatest of two number using conditional operator

```c
/* Greatest Number */
#include<stdio.h>
#include<conio.h>
void main()
{
int a,b;
clrscr();
printf("Enter the values: ");
scanf("%d %d",&a,&b);
(a>b)?printf("\nFirst number is greater"):printf("\nSecond number is greater");
getch();}
```

```
/*----------------------------------
Output:
Enter the values: 56 78
Second number is greater
------------------------------------*/
```

12. Program to find the biggest of three numbers

```c
/* Biggest of three numbers*/
#include <stdio.h>
#include <conio.h>
#include <math.h>
void main()
{
int a, b, c;
clrscr();
printf("Enter the values of a,b and c\n");
scanf ("%d %d %d", &a, &b, &c);
printf ("a = %d\tb = %d\tc = %d\n", a,b,c);
if ( a > b)
{
if ( a > c)
{
printf ("A is the greatest among three\n");
}
else
{
printf ("C is the greatest among three\n");
}
}
else if (b > c)
{
printf ("B is the greatest among three\n");
}
else
printf ("C is the greatest among three\n");
getch();
}
```

```
/*----------------------------------
Output:
Enter the values of a,b and c
23 32 45
a = 23  b = 32  c = 45
C is the greatest among three
--------------------------------------*/
```

13. Program to swap the given two numbers using bitwise operator

```
/* Swapping using bitwise operator */
#include <stdio.h>
#include<conio.h>
void main()
{
long i,k;
clrscr();
printf("Enter two integers\n");
scanf("%ld %ld",&i,&k);
printf("\nBefore swapping i= %ld and k = %ld",i,k);
i = i^k;
k = i^k;
i = i^k;
printf("\nAfter swapping i= %ld and k = %ld",i,k);
getch();
}

/*---------------------------------------------
Output:
Enter two integers
23 34
Before swapping i= 23 and k = 34
After swapping i= 34 and k = 23
-------------------------------------------------*/
```

14. Program(Magic Number Game) to illustrate the usage of rand() function

```c
/* Find the magic number */
#include<stdio.h>
#include<conio.h>
void main()
{
int magic,guess,i,score;
clrscr();
magic=rand();
i=0;
do
{
printf("\n\nGuess the magic number: ");
scanf("%d",&guess);
if(guess==magic)
{
printf("====Correct Answer===\n");
printf("%d is the magic number",magic);
}
else if(guess>magic)
{++i;
printf("***Wrong Answer(Too High)***");
}
else
{++i;
printf("***Wrong Answer(Too Small)***");
}
}while((i<10)&&(guess!=magic));
score=(10-i)*10;
printf("\n\nScore: You got %d out of 100",score);
getch();
}

/*---------------------------------
Output:
Guess the magic number: 5000
***Wrong Answer(Too High)***
```

```
Guess the magic number: 300
***Wrong Answer(Too Small)***

Guess the magic number: 346
===Correct Answer===
346 is the magic number

Score: You got 80 out of 100
-----------------------------------*/
```

15. Program to illustrate the floor(), ceil(), fabs() functions

```c
/* Illustrate the floor(), ceil(), fabs() function */
#include<stdio.h>
#include<conio.h>
#include<math.h>
void main()
{
float num;
clrscr();
printf("Enter a float value:\n");
scanf("%f",&num);
printf("The given value using floor():  %f\n",floor(num));
printf("The given value using ceil():  %f\n",ceil(num));
printf("The given value using fabs():  %f\n",fabs(num));
getch();
}

/*-----------------------------------------------------------
Output:
Enter a float value:
23.145
The given value using floor():  23.000000
The given value using ceil() :  24.000000
The given value using fabs() :  24.145000
-----------------------------------------------------------*/
```

16. Program to convert the Fahrenheit temperature to Celsius

```c
/*Fahrenheit to Celsius*/
#include<stdio.h>
#include<conio.h>
void main()
{
float fah,cel;
clrscr();
printf("Enter the temperature in Fahrenheit:\n");
scanf("%f",&fah);
cel=(fah-32.0)/1.8;
printf("The equivalent temperature in Celsius:\n");
printf("%5.2f",cel);
getch();
}


/*-------------------------------------------------
Output:
Enter the temperature in Fahrenheit:
250
The equivalent temperature in Celsius:
121.11
-----------------------------------------------------*/
```

17. Program to solve the given quadratic equation

```c
/* Program to solve quadratic equation */
#include <stdio.h>
#include <conio.h>
#include <stdlib.h>
#include <math.h>
void main()
{
float a, b, c, root1, root2;
float real, imag, disc;
clrscr();
printf("Enter the values of a, b and c\n");
```

```c
scanf("%f %f %f", &a,&b,&c);
if( a==0 || b==0 || c==0)
{
printf("Unable to determine the roots: Error\n");
exit(1);
}
else
{
disc = b*b - 4.0*a*c;
if(disc < 0)
{
printf("Roots are Imaginary\n");
real = -b/(2.0*a) ;
imag = sqrt(abs(disc))/(2.0*a);
printf("root1 = %f  +i %f\n",real, imag);
printf("root2 = %f  -i %f\n",real, imag);
}
else if(disc == 0)
{
printf("Roots are Real and Equal\n");
root1 = -b/(2.0*a);
root2 = root1;
printf("The root1 = %f  \n",root1);
printf("The root2 = %f  \n",root2);
}
else if(disc > 0 )
{
printf("Roots are Real and Distinct\n");
root1 =(-b+sqrt(disc))/(2.0*a);
root2 =(-b-sqrt(disc))/(2.0*a);
printf("The root1 = %f  \n",root1);
printf("The root2 = %f  \n",root2);
}
}
getch();
}
```

```
/*---------------------------------------
Output:
Enter the values of a, b and c
3 2 1
The roots are Imaginary
The root1 = -0.333333  +i 0.471405
The root2 = -0.333333  -i 0.471405

Enter the values of a, b and c
1 2 1
Roots are Real and Equal
The root1 = -1.000000
The root2 = -1.000000

Enter the values of a, b and c
3 5 2
Roots are Real and Distinct
The root1 = -0.666667
The root2 = -1.000000
------------------------------------------*/
```

18. Program to find the factorial of a given number

```
/* Factorial */
#include <stdio.h>
#include<conio.h>
void main()
{
int  i,fact=1,num;
clrscr();
printf("Enter the number\n");
scanf("%d",&num);
if( num <= 0)
fact = 1;
else
{
for(i = 1; i <= num; i++)
{
```

```
            fact = fact * i;
        }
    }
    printf("Factorial of %d =%5d\n", num,fact);
    getch();
}


/*-------------------------------------------
Output:
Enter the number
5
Factorial of 5 =  120
---------------------------------------------*/
```

19. Program to find the quadrant of operation for the given co-ordinates

```
/* Quadrant operation*/
#include <stdio.h>
#include<conio.h>
void main()
{
int x,y;
clrscr();
printf("Enter the values for X and Y\n");
scanf("%d %d",&x,&y);
if( x > 0 && y > 0)
printf("point (%d,%d) lies in the First quadrant\n");
else if( x < 0 && y > 0)
printf("point (%d,%d) lies in the Second quadrant\n");
else if( x < 0 && y < 0)
printf("point (%d, %d) lies in the Third quadrant\n");
else if( x > 0 && y < 0)
printf("point (%d,%d) lies in the Fourth quadrant\n");
else if( x == 0 && y == 0)
printf("point (%d,%d) lies at the origin\n");
getch();
}
```

```
/*--------------------------------------------
Output:
Enter the values for X and Y
3 5
point (5,3) lies in the First quadrant
---------------------------------------------*/
```

20. Program to convert the lower case character into upper case (vice versa)

```c
/* Lower case to Upper case (vice versa) */
#include<stdio.h>
#include<conio.h>
#include<ctype.h>
void main()
{
char alpha;
clrscr();
printf("Enter an alphabet: ");
alpha=getchar();
if(islower(alpha)){
printf("The char is lower case. So, :");
putchar(toupper(alpha));
}
else{
printf("The char is upper case. So, :");
putchar(tolower(alpha));
}
getch();
}

/*------------------------------------
Output:
Enter an alphabet: a
The char is lower case. So, :A
Enter an alphabet: A
The char is upper case. So, :a
-------------------------------------*/
```

21. Program to find whether a given character is alphanumeric

```
/* Find alphanumeric or not */
#include<stdio.h>
#include<conio.h>
#include<ctype.h>
void main()
{
char character;
clrscr();
printf("Enter any character:\n");
character=getchar();
if(isalpha(character)>0)
printf("Yes... It is an alphabet");
else if(isdigit(character)>0)
printf("Yes... It is a digit");
else
printf("The character is not an alphanumeric");
getch();}


/*--------------------------------------------------
Output:
Enter any character:
A
Yes... It is an alphabet

Enter any character:
6
Yes... It is a digit

Enter any character:
*
The character is not an alphanumeric
----------------------------------------------------*/
```

22. Program to perform basic arithmetic operations using switch statement

```c
/* Basic arithmetic operations*/
#include<stdio.h>
#include<conio.h>
void main()
{
int a,b,c,d;
clrscr();
printf("Enter the input value:\n");
scanf("%d %d",&a,&b);
printf("Option Menu:\n 1.Addition\n 2.Subtraction\n 3.Multiplication\n 4.Division\n");
printf("Enter your Option:\t");
scanf("%d",&d);
switch(d)
{
case 1:
c=a+b;
printf("The Addition Value: %d",c);
break;
case 2:
c=a-b;
printf("The Subtraction Value: %d",c);
break;
case 3:
c=a*b;
printf("The Mulitiplication value: %d",c);
break;
case 4:
c=a/b;
printf("The division vaue: %d",c);
}
getch();
}
```

```
/*----------------------------------------
Output:
Enter the input value:
5 5
Option Menu:
  1.Addition
  2.Subtraction
  3.Multiplication
  4.Division
Enter your Option:    3
The Mulitiplication value: 25
------------------------------------------*/
```

23. Program to fin the GCD and LCM of two integers

```c
/* GCD and LCM */
#include <stdio.h>
#include <conio.h>
void main()
{
int  num1, num2, gcd, lcm, remainder, numerator, denominator;
clrscr();
printf("Enter two numbers\n");
scanf("%d %d", &num1,&num2);
if (num1 > num2)
{
numerator = num1;
denominator = num2;
}
else
{
numerator = num2;
denominator = num1;
}
remainder = num1 % num2;
while(remainder !=0)
{
numerator   = denominator;
```

```
denominator = remainder;
remainder   = numerator % denominator;
}
gcd = denominator;
lcm = num1 * num2 / gcd;
printf("GCD of %d and %d = %d \n", num1,num2,gcd);
printf("LCM of %d and %d = %d \n", num1,num2,lcm);
getch();
}


/*---------------------------
Output:
Enter two numbers
5
15
GCD of 5 and 15 = 5
LCM of 5 and 15 = 15
------------------------------*/
```

24. Program to generate fibonacci numbers

```
/* Fibonacci numbers*/
#include <stdio.h>
#include<conio.h>
void main()
{
int   fib1=0, fib2=1, fib3, N, count=0;
clrscr();
printf("Enter the value of N\n");
scanf("%d", &N);
printf("First %d FIBONACCI numbers are ...\n", N);
printf("%d\n",fib1);
printf("%d\n",fib2);
count = 2;
while( count < N)
{
fib3 = fib1 + fib2;
count ++;
```

```
        printf("%d\n",fib3);
        fib1 = fib2;
        fib2 = fib3;
        }
        getch();
        }


        /*----------------------------------------
        Enter the value of N
        10
        First 5 fibonacci numbers are ...
        0 1 1 2 3 5 8 13 21 34
        --------------------------------------------*/
```

25. Program to check whether the given number is palindrome or not

```
        /* Find palindrome or not*/
        #include <stdio.h>
        #include <conio.h>
        void main()
        {
        int   num, temp, digit, rev = 0;
        clrscr();
        printf("Enter an integer\n");
        scanf("%d", &num);
        temp = num;
        while(num > 0)
        {
        digit = num % 10;
        rev = rev * 10 + digit;
        num /= 10;
        }
        printf("Given number is = %d\n", temp);
        printf("Its reverse is  = %d\n", rev);
        if(temp == rev )
        printf("Number is a palindrome\n");
        else
        printf("Number is not a palindrome\n");
```

```
getch();
}
```

```
/*--------------------------------
Output:
Enter an integer
12321
Given number is = 12321
Its reverse is = 12321
Number is a palindrome

Enter an integer
3456
Given number is = 3456
Its reverse is = 6543
Number is not a palindrome
-----------------------------------*/
```

26. Program to accept an integer and find the sum of the digits in it

```
/* Sum of the digits */
#include <stdio.h>
#include<conio.h>
void main()
{
long num, temp, digit, sum = 0;
printf("Enter the number\n");
scanf("%ld", &num);
temp = num;
while(num > 0)
{
digit = num % 10;
sum  = sum + digit;
num /= 10;
}
printf("Given number =%ld\n", temp);
printf("Sum of the digits %ld =%ld\n", temp, sum);
getch();}
```

```
/*----------------------------------------
Output:
Enter the number
123456
Given number =123456
Sum of the digits 123456 =21
-----------------------------------------*/
```

27. Program to perform the logical XNOR operation

```c
/*Logical XNOR operation*/
#include<stdio.h>
#include<conio.h>
int xnor(int a,int b);
void main()
{
int a,b,y;
clrscr();
printf("Enter the inputs( 0 or 1): ");
scanf("%d %d",&a,&b);
y=xnor(a,b);
printf("\nThe XNOR gate output: %d",y);
getch();
}

int xnor(int a,int b)
{
return (!((a||b) && !(a&&b)));
}


/*----------------------------------------
Output:
Enter the inputs(0 or 1): 1 0
The XNOR gate output: 0
-----------------------------------------*/
```

28. Program to calculate the compound interest

```c
/* Compound Interest */
#include<stdio.h>
#include<conio.h>
#include<math.h>
void main()
{
float sum,period,rate,amount,com_int;
int n;
clrscr();
printf("Enter the values for sum, period and rate:\n");
scanf("%f %f %f",&sum,&period,&rate);
printf("\nOptions: \n1.Annually Compounded\n2.Half-yearly Compounded\n3.Quarterly Compounded\n");
printf("\nEnter the type of compound interest: ");
scanf("%d",&n);

switch(n)
{
case 1:
{
amount=sum*(pow((1+0.01*rate),period));
com_int=amount-sum;
break;
}
case 2:
{
amount=sum*(pow((1+0.005*rate),(2.0*period)));
com_int=amount-sum;
break;
}
case 3:
{
amount=sum*(pow((1+0.025*rate),(4.0*period)));
com_int=amount-sum;
break;
}
```

```
default:
printf("Enter valid option:\n");
}
printf("\nThe compound interest: %f\n",com_int);
printf("The total amount    : %f",amount);
getch();
}



/*-----------------------------------------
Output:
Enter the values for sum, period and rate:
6250 2 16
Options:
1.Annually Compounded
2.Half-yearly Compounded
3.Quarterly Compounded

Enter the type of compound interest: 1
The compound interest: 2160.000000
The total amount    : 8410.000000
-------------------------------------------*/
```

29. Program to understand the usage of bitwise operator

```
/* Usage of Bitwise Operator */
#include<stdio.h>
#include<conio.h>
void main()
{
int i,j;
clrscr();
i=1;
for(j=0;j<4;j++)
{
i=i<<1;
printf("Left shift %d: %d\n",j+1,i);
}
printf("\n");
```

```
for(j=0;j<4;j++)
{
i=i>>1;
printf("Right shift %d: %d\n",j+1,i);
}
getch();
}


/*----------------------------------
Output:
Left shift 1: 2
Left shift 2: 4
Left shift 3: 8
Left shift 4: 16

Right shift 1: 8
Right shift 2: 4
Right shift 3: 2
Right shift 4: 1
------------------------------------*/
```

30. Program to perform mark analysis using if else statement

```
/* Program to perform mark analysis */
#include<stdio.h>
#include<conio.h>
void main()
{
int mark1,mark2,mark3,total,grade;
float avg;
clrscr();
printf("Enter the 3 subject marks:\n");
scanf("%d %d %d",&mark1,&mark2,&mark3);
total=mark1+mark2+mark3;
avg=total/3;
printf("The total mark: %d\n",total);
printf("The average mark: %f\n",avg);
if(avg>79)
```

```
        grade=1;
        else if(avg>59)
        grade=2;
        else if(avg>49)
        grade=3;
        else if(avg>=35)
        grade=4;
        else
        grade=0;
        if(grade==0)
        printf("The student got fail mark\n");
        else
        printf("The student get %d class",grade);
        getch();
        }


        /*----------------------------------------
        Output:
        Enter the 3 subject marks:
        67
        78
        89
        The total mark: 234
        The average mark: 78.000000
        The student get 2 class
        -----------------------------------------*/
```

31. Program to generate the prime numbers within the given limits

```
        /* Generate the prime numbers */
        #include <stdio.h>
        #include <conio.h>
        #include <stdlib.h>
        #include <math.h>
        void main()
        {
        int low, up, i, j, flag, temp, count = 0;
        clrscr();
```

```c
printf("Enter the value of lower and upper limits:\n");
scanf("%d %d", &low,&up);
if(up < 2)
{
printf("There are no primes upto %d\n", up);
exit(0);
}
printf("The prime numbers are\n");
temp = low;
if ( low % 2 == 0)
{
low++;
}
for (i=low; i<=up; i=i+2)
{
flag = 0;
for (j=2; j<=i/2; j++)
{
if( (i%j) == 0)
{
flag = 1;
break;
}
}
if(flag == 0)
{
printf("%d\n",i);
count++;
}
}
printf("Number of prime numbers between %d and %d = %d\n",temp,up,count);
getch();
}

/*------------------------------------------------------------
Output:
Enter the value of lower and upper limits:
```

```
15 45
The prime numbers are
17
19
23
29
31
37
41
43
Number of primes between 15 and 45 = 8
------------------------------------------------------------*/
```

32. Program to search an element in an array

```c
/* Searching using arrays*/
#include<stdio.h>
#include<conio.h>
void main()
{
int array[10];
int i,N,keynum,found=0;
clrscr();
printf("Enter the limit:\n");
scanf("%d",&N);
printf("Enter the elements:\n");
for(i=0;i<N;i++)
{
scanf("%d",&array[i]);
}
printf("Enter the element to be searched:\n");
scanf("%d",&keynum);
for(i=0;i<N;i++)
{
if(keynum==array[i])
{
found=1;
break;
```

```
}
}
if(found==1)
printf("Successful search\n");
else
printf("Search is failed\n");
getch();
}

/*------------------------------------------
Output:
Enter the limit:
5
Enter the elements:
45 56 32 78 54
Enter the element to be searched:
32
Successful search

Enter the limit:
5
Enter the elements:
45 56 32 78 54
Enter the element to be searched:
28
Search is failed
----------------------------------------------*/
```

33. Program to calculate the median using arrays

```
/*Program to calculate the median using arrays*/
#include<stdio.h>
#include<conio.h>
#define N 10
void main()
{
int i,j,n;
float median,a[N],t;
```

```c
clrscr();
printf("Enter the limit:\n");
scanf("%d",&n);
printf("Enter %d values:\n",n);
for(i=1;i<=n;i++)
scanf("%f",&a[i]);
for(i=1;i<=n-1;i++)
{
for(j=1;j<=n-i;j++)
{
if(a[j]<=a[j+1])
{
t=a[j];
a[j]=a[j+1];
a[j+1]=t;
}
else
continue;
}
}
if(n%2==0)
median=(a[n/2] + a[n/2+1])/2.0;
else
median=a[n/2+1];
printf("\nThe sorted list:\n");
for(i=1;i<=n;i++)
printf("%f ",a[i]);
printf("\n\nThe median is: %f\n",median);
getch();
}

/*----------------------------------------
Output:
Enter the limit:
4
Enter 4 values:
5 6 7 8
```

The sorted list:
8.000000 7.000000 6.000000 5.000000

The median is: 6.500000
--*/

34. Program to find the biggest of 10 numbers

```c
/* Program to find the biggest of 10 numbers */
#include<stdio.h>
#include<conio.h>
void main()
{
int element[10],i,big=0;
clrscr();
printf("Enter the values:");
for(i=0;i<10;i++)
scanf("%d",&element[i]);
big=element[0];
for(i=0;i<10;i++)
if(big<element[i])
big=element[i];
printf("The biggest number is: %d",big);
getch();
}
```

/*--
Output:
Enter the values: 10 2 6 4 3 6 7 9 1 8
The biggest number is: 10
--*/

35. Program to produce the multiplication table using for loop

```c
/* Multiplication table using for loop*/
#include<stdio.h>
#include<conio.h>
void main()
```

```c
{
int row,column,y;
clrscr();
printf("Multiplication Table\n\n");
for(row=1;row<=10;row++)
{
for(column=1;column<=12;column++)
{
y=row*column;
printf("%4d",y);
}
printf("\n");
}
getch();
}
```

```
/*------------------------------------------------------
Output:
Multiplication Table

   1   2   3   4   5   6   7   8   9  10  11  12
   2   4   6   8  10  12  14  16  18  20  22  24
   3   6   9  12  15  18  21  24  27  30  33  36
   4   8  12  16  20  24  28  32  36  40  44  48
   5  10  15  20  25  30  35  40  45  50  55  60
   6  12  18  24  30  36  42  48  54  60  66  72
   7  14  21  28  35  42  49  56  63  70  77  84
   8  16  24  32  40  48  56  64  72  80  88  96
   9  18  27  36  45  54  63  72  81  90  99 108
  10  20  30  40  50  60  70  80  90 100 110 120
------------------------------------------------------*/
```

36. Program to calculate the mean, variance and standard deviation

```c
/*Calculate the mean, variance, standard deviation */
#include <stdio.h>
#include <conio.h>
#include <math.h>
```

```c
void main()
{
float x[10];
int i,n;
float mean,vari,std_dev,sum=0,sum1=0;
clrscr();
printf("Enter the limit:\n");
scanf("%d",&n);
printf("Enter %d real numbers:\n",n);
for(i=0;i<n;i++)
{
scanf("%f",&x[i]);
}
for(i=0;i<n;i++)
{
sum = sum + x[i];
}
mean = sum /(float) n;
for(i=0; i<n; i++)
{
sum1 = sum1 + pow((x[i] - mean),2);
}
vari = sum1 / (float) n;
std_dev = sqrt(vari);
printf("The Mean of all elements  = %.2f\n", mean);
printf("The Varience of all elements = %.2f\n", vari);
printf("The Standard deviation     = %.2f\n", std_dev);
getch();
}

/*--------------------------
Output:
Enter the limit:
5
Enter 5 real numbers
10
20
30
```

40
50
The Mean of all elements = 30.00
The Varience of all elements = 200.00
The Standard deviation   = 14.14
-------------------------------------*/

37. Program to find the largest number from two dimensional array using functions

```
/* Largest Number in two dimensional array*/
#include<stdio.h>
#include<conio.h>
#define M 2
#define N 2
float largest(float a[][N],int,int);
void main()
{
float a[2][2],y;
int i,j;
clrscr();
printf("Enter the values: ");
for(i=0;i<2;i++)
for(j=0;j<2;j++)
scanf("%f",&a[i][j]);
y=largest(a,M,N);
printf("The largest Number: %f",y);
getch();
}

float largest(float a[][N],int m, int n)
{
float max;
int i,j;
max=a[0][0];
for(i=0;i<m;i++)
for(j=0;j<n;j++)
if(max<a[i][j])
```

```
max=a[i][j];
return(max);
}
```

```
/*---------------------------------------
Output::
Enter the values: 56 67 78 54
The largest Number: 78.000000
----------------------------------------*/
```

38. Program to find the factorial using recursion

```
/* Factorial using recursion */
#include<stdio.h>
#include<conio.h>
int factorial(int);
void main()
{
int y,n,a;
clrscr();
do
{
printf("Enter the value for factorial: ");
scanf("%d",&n);
y=factorial(n);
printf("The factorial value: %d",y);
printf("\nEnter 1 for continue:");
scanf("%d",&a);
}
while(a==1);
getch();
}

int factorial(int n)
{
int fact;
if(n==1)
return(1);
```

```
else
{
fact=n*factorial(n-1);
return(fact);
}
}


/*-------------------------------------
Output:
Enter the value for factorial: 5
The factorial value: 120
Enter 1 for continue:0
----------------------------------------*/
```

39. Program to perform basic arithmetic operations using functions

```
/*Program to perform basic arithmetic operations using functions */
#include<stdio.h>
#include<conio.h>
float mul(float,float);
float add(float,float);
float div(float,float);
void main()
{
float x,y,z;
clrscr();
x=add(100,25);
printf("The Addition value: %f\n",x);
y=mul(10.5,5.0);
printf("The Multiplication value: %f\n",y);
z=div(25,5);
printf("The division value: %f\n",z);
getch();
}

float add(float a,float b)
{
return(a+b);
```

}
float mul(float c,float d)
{
return(c*d);
}
float div(float q,float p)
{
return(q/p);
}

/*------------------------------------
Output:
The Addition value: 125.000000
The Multiplication value: 52.500000
The division value: 5.000000
--*/

40. Program to use nesting of functions

```
/* Nesting of fuctions */
#include<stdio.h>
#include<conio.h>
float mul(float,float);
void main()
{
float y;
clrscr();
y=mul(mul(10.5,5.0),3);
printf("The Multiplication Value: %f",y);
getch();
}

float mul(float c,float d)
{
return(c*d);
}
```

```
/*----------------------------------------
Output:
The Multiplication Value: 157.500000
-------------------------------------------*/
```

41. Program to read a line of text and reverse it using recursive function

```c
/*Reading a line of text and reverse it using recursive function*/
#include<stdio.h>
#include<conio.h>
void reversed_text(void);
void main()
{
clrscr();
printf("Enter the text:\n");
reverse();
getch();
}
void reversed_text(void)
{
char ch;
if((ch=getchar())!='\n')
reversed_text();
putchar(ch);
return;
}

/*----------------------------------------
Output:
Enter the text:
Venkatesh

hsetakneV
-------------------------------------------*/
```

42. Program to find the largest number using function

```c
/* Largest Number using Functions */
#include<stdio.h>
#include<conio.h>
float largest(float a[],int n);
void main()
{
float a[10],y;
int i,lim;
clrscr();
printf("Enter the limit:\n);
scanf("%d",&lim);
printf("Enter the values: ");
for(i=0;i<lim;i++)
scanf("%f",&a[i]);
y=largest(a,lim);
printf("The largest Number: %f",y);
getch();
}

float largest(float a[], int n)
{
float max;
int i;
max=a[0];
for(i=1;i<n;i++)
if(max<a[i])
max=a[i];
return(max);}

/*-----------------------------------------
Output:
Enter the limit:
5
Enter the values: 45 65 78 99 23
The largest Number: 99.000000
------------------------------------------*/
```

43. Program to produce Towers of Hanoi

```c
/*Towers of Hanoi*/
#include<stdio.h>
#include<conio.h>
void transfer(int n,char from,char to,char temp);
void main()
{
int n;
clrscr();
printf("Towers of Hanoi\n");
printf("---------------\n");
printf("Enter the number of disks:  ");
scanf("%d",&n);
printf("\n");
transfer(n,'L','R','C');
getch();
}

void transfer(int n,char from,char to,char temp)
{
if(n>0)
{
transfer(n-1,from,temp,to);
printf("Move disk %d from %c to %c\n",n,from,to);
transfer(n-1,temp,to,from);
}
return;
}

/*-----------------------------------
Output:
Towers of Hanoi
---------------
Enter the number of disks: 3

Move disk 1 from L to R
Move disk 2 from L to C
```

Move disk 1 from R to C
Move disk 3 from L to R
Move disk 1 from C to L
Move disk 2 from C to R
Move disk 1 from L to R
--------------------------------------*/

44. Program to find the sum of series (1+2+3+....+N) using recursive function

```
/* Sum of series 1+2+3+.....+n using recursive function */
#include<stdio.h>
#include<conio.h>
int funct(int);
void main()
{
int n;
clrscr();
printf("Enter the limit: ");
scanf("%d",&n);
printf("The sum of series 1+2+3+.....+n: %d",funct(n));
getch();
}
int funct(int n)
{
if(n>0)
return(n+funct(n-1));
}

/*--------------------------------------
Output:
Enter the limit: 10
The sum of series 1+2+3+.....+n: 55
--------------------------------------*/
```

45. Program to convert the given decimal number into binary number

```c
/* Decimal number into Binary number */
#include<stdio.h>
#include<conio.h>
void main()
{
long num,deci,rem,base=1,bin=0;
clrscr();
printf("Enter a decimal integer\n");
scanf("%ld",&num);
deci=num;
while(num>0)
{
rem=num%2;
bin=bin+rem*base;
num=num/2;
base=base*10;
}
printf("Input number is: %ld\n",deci);
printf("Its binary equivalent is: %ld\n",bin);
getch();
}

/*-----------------------------------------
Output:
Enter a decimal number:
10
Input number is: 10
Its binary equivalent is: 1010
------------------------------------------*/
```

46. Program to convert the given octal number into decimal number

```c
/* Octal number into Decimal number*/
#include<stdio.h>
#include<conio.h>
void main()
```

```c
{
int deci=0,base=1,rem,oct,num;
clrscr();
printf("Enter a octal number:\n");
scanf("%d",&num);
oct=num;
while(num>0)
{
rem=num%10;
deci=deci+rem*base;
num=num/10;
base=base*8;
}
printf("The input octal number is: %ld\n",oct);
printf("Its decimal equivalent is: %d\n",deci);
getch();
}


/*---------------------------------------------
Output:
Enter a octal number:
4706
The input octal number is: 4706
Its decimal equivalent is: 2502
---------------------------------------------*/
```

46. Program to convert the given binary number into decimal number

```c
/* Binary number into Decimal number*/
#include<stdio.h>
#include<conio.h>
void main()
{
int deci=0,base=1,rem;
long bin,num;
clrscr();
printf("Enter a binary number:\n");
scanf("%ld",&num);
```

```
bin=num;

while(num>0)
{
rem=num%10;
deci=deci+rem*base;
num=num/10;
base=base*2;
}
printf("The input binary number is: %ld\n",bin);
printf("Its decimal equivalent is: %d\n",deci);
getch();
}


/*--------------------------------------------
Output:
Enter a binary number:
1010
The input binary number is: 1010
Its decimal equivalent is: 10
----------------------------------------------*/
```

48. Program to convert the given decimal number into octal number

```
/* Decimal number into Octal number */
#include<stdio.h>
#include<conio.h>
void main()
{
long num,deci,rem,base=1,oct=0;
clrscr();
printf("Enter a decimal integer\n");
scanf("%ld",&num);
deci=num;
while(num>0)
{
rem=num%8;
oct=oct+rem*base;
```

```
num=num/8;
base=base*10;
}
printf("Input decimal number is: %ld\n",deci);
printf("Its octal equivalent is: %ld\n",oct);
getch();
}
```

```
/*-------------------------------------------
Output:
Enter a decimal number: 952
Input decimal number is: 952
Its octal equivalent is: 1670
-----------------------------------------*/
```

49. Program to convert the given binary number into octal number

```
/* Binary number into Octal number */
#include<stdio.h>
#include<conio.h>
void main()
{
int deci=0,oct=0,base=1,basee=1,rem;
long bin,num;
clrscr();
printf("Enter a binary number:\n");
scanf("%ld",&num);
bin=num;
while(num>0)
{
rem=num%10;
deci=deci+rem*base;
num=num/10;
base=base*2;
}
while(deci>0)
{
rem=deci%8;
```

```
oct=oct+rem*basee;
deci=deci/8;
basee=basee*10;
}
printf("The input binary number: %ld\n",bin);
printf("Its equivalent octal number is: %d",oct);
getch();
}
```

```
/*----------------------------------------
Output:
Enter a binary number:
101110
The input binary number: 101110
Its equivalent octal number is: 56
-----------------------------------------*/
```

50. Program to perform Bubble Sort

```
/*Bubble Sort*/
#include<stdio.h>
#include<conio.h>
void main()
{
int n,i,j,a[25],temp;
clrscr();
printf("Enter the Limit value:\t");
scanf("%d",&n);
printf("Enter the elements:");
for(i=0;i<n;i++)
scanf("%d",&a[i]);
for(i=0;i<=n-1;i++)
{
for(j=i+1;j<=n-1;j++)
if(a[i]>a[j])
{
temp=a[i];
a[i]=a[j];
```

```
a[j]=temp;
}
}
printf("The sorted list is:");
for(i=0;i<n;i++)
printf("%d  ",a[i]);
getch();
}
```

```
/*------------------------------------------
Output:
Enter the Limit value:  8
Enter the elements:
5 3 7 5 9 4 10 6
The sorted list is:3  4  5  5  6  7  9  10
--------------------------------------------*/
```

51. Program to perform Selection Sort

```
/*Selection Sort*/
#include<stdio.h>
#include<conio.h>
void main()
{
int n,i,j,k,min,a[25];
clrscr();
printf("Enter the Limit value:\t");
scanf("%d",&n);
printf("Enter the elements:");
for(i=0;i<n;i++)
scanf("%d",&a[i]);
for(i=0;i<=n-1;i++)
{
k=i;
min=a[i];
for(j=i+1;j<=n-1;j++)
if(a[j]<min)
{
```

```
min=a[j];
k=j;
}
a[k]=a[i];
a[i]=min;
}
printf("The sorted list is:");
for(i=0;i<n;i++)
printf("%d ",a[i]);
getch();
}


/*------------------------------------------
Output:
Enter the Limit value:  8
Enter the elements:
5 3 7 5 9 4 10 6
The sorted list is:3  4  5  5  6  7  9  10
----------------------------------------------*/
```

52. Program to perform the Insertion Sort

```
/*Insertion Sort*/
#include<stdio.h>
#include<conio.h>
void main()
{
int n,i,j,a[25],temp;
clrscr();
printf("Enter the Limit value:\t");
scanf("%d",&n);
printf("Enter the elements:");
for(i=0;i<n;i++)
scanf("%d",&a[i]);
for(i=1;i<=n-1;i++)
{
temp=a[i];
for(j=i;j>=1;j--)
```

```
{
if(temp<a[j-1])
a[j]=a[j-1];
else
break;
}
a[j]=temp;
}
printf("The sorted list is:");
for(i=0;i<n;i++)
printf("%d  ",a[i]);
getch();
}


/*-------------------------------------------
Output:
Enter the Limit value:  8
Enter the elements:
5 3 7 5 9 4 10 6
The sorted list is:3  4  5  5  6  7  9  10
---------------------------------------------*/
```

53. Program to produce the following output:

```
*
**
***
****
*****
```

```c
#include<stdio.h>
#include<conio.h>
void main()
{
int i,j;
clrscr();
for(i=1;i<=5;i++)
{
for(j=1;j<=i;j++)
```

```
    {
    printf("*");
    }
    printf("\n");
    }
    getch();
}

/*------------
Output:
*
**
***
****
*****
--------------*/
```

54. Program to produce the following output:
```
    1
   22
  333
 4444
55555
```

```c
#include<stdio.h>
#include<conio.h>
void main()
{
int i,j,count,k;
clrscr();
count=5;
for(i=1;i<=5;i++)
{
for(k=count-1;k>=1;--k)
printf(" ");
for(j=1;j<=i;j++)
{
printf("%d",i);
```

}
count-=1;
printf("\n");
}
getch();
}

/*----------------
Output:
```
    1
   22
  333
 4444
55555
```
------------------*/

55. Program to produce the following output:
```
   1
  23
 456
78910
```

```c
#include<stdio.h>
#include<conio.h>
void main()
{
int i,j,incre,count,k;
clrscr();
incre=0;
count=5;
for(i=1;i<=4;i++)
{
for(k=count-1;k>=1;--k)
printf(" ");
for(j=1;j<=i;j++)
{
printf("%d",++incre);
}
```

```
count-=1;
printf("\n");
}
getch();
}


/*-------------------
Output:
    1
   23
  456
 78910
--------------------*/
```

56. Program to produce the following output:

```
    *
   ***
  *****
 *******
*********
```

```c
#include<stdio.h>
#include<conio.h>
void main()
{
int i,j,count,k,l;
clrscr();
count=5;
l=0;
for(i=1;i<=5;i++)
{
for(k=count-1;k>=1;--k)
printf(" ");
for(j=1;j<=i+l;j++)
{
printf("*");
}
count-=1;
```

```
l+=1;
printf("\n");
}
getch();
}


/*------------------
Output:
       *
     ***
    *****
   *******
  *********
--------------------*/
```

57. Program to produce the following output:
```
* $ $ $ $
$ * $ $ $
$ $ * $ $
$ $ $ * $
$ $ $ $ *
```

```c
#include<stdio.h>
#include<conio.h>
void main()
{
int i,j;
clrscr();
for(i=0;i<5;i++)
{
for(j=0;j<5;j++)
{
if(i==j)
printf("* ");
else
printf("$ ");
}
printf("\n");
```

```
}
getch();
}


/*------------------
Output:
* $ $ $ $
$ * $ $ $
$ $ * $ $
$ $ $ * $
$ $ $ $ *
--------------------*/
```

58. Program to produce the following output:

```
# # # # #
# # # # #
# # 0 # #
# # # # #
# # # # #
```

```c
#include<stdio.h>
#include<conio.h>
void main()
{
int i,j;
clrscr();
for(i=0;i<5;i++)
{
for(j=0;j<5;j++)
{
if(i==2&&j==2)
printf("0 ");
else
printf("# ");
}
printf("\n");
}
getch();}
```

```
/*------------------
Output:
# # # # #
# # # # #
# # 0 # #
# # # # #
# # # # #
-------------------*/
```

59. Program to produce the following output:
```
    1
   234
  56789
```

```c
#include<stdio.h>
#include<conio.h>
void main()
{
int i,j,count,k,l,incre;
clrscr();
count=3;
l=0;
incre=0;
for(i=1;i<=3;i++)
{
for(k=count-1;k>=1;--k)
printf(" ");
for(j=1;j<=i+l;j++)
{
printf("%d",++incre);
}
count-=1;
l+=1;
printf("\n");
}
getch();
}
```

```
/*------------------------
Output:
  1
   234
56789
-------------------------*/
```

60. Program to perform mark analysis using structures

```c
/* program to calculate the total marks and average */
#include<stdio.h>
#include<conio.h>
struct marks
{
int sub1;
int sub2;
int sub3;
int total;
float avg;
};
void main()
{
int i,grade;
struct marks stu[3];
clrscr();
for(i=0;i<3;i++)
{
printf("Enter the marks of %d th student:\n",i+1);
scanf("%d %d %d",&stu[i].sub1,&stu[i].sub2,&stu[i].sub3);
}
for(i=0;i<3;i++)
{
stu[i].total=stu[i].sub1+stu[i].sub2+stu[i].sub3;
stu[i].avg=stu[i].total/3;
if(stu[i].avg>60)
grade=1;
else if(stu[i].avg>50)
grade=2;
```

```c
else if(stu[i].avg>40)
grade=3;
else if(stu[i].avg<35)
grade=0;
if(grade==0)
printf("The %d student got fail mark\n",i+1);
else
printf("The %d student got %d grade\n",i+1,grade);
printf("The total marks of %d th student: %d\n",i+1,stu[i].total);
printf("The average of %d th student: %f\n\n\n",i+1,stu[i].avg);
}
getch();
}
```

/*--
Output:
Enter the marks of 1 th student:
56
56
56
Enter the marks of 2 th student:
78
78
78
Enter the marks of 3 th student:
23
23
23

The 1 student got 2 grade
The total marks of 1 th student: 168.00
The average of the 1 th student: 55.00

The 2 student got 1 grade
The total marks of 2 th student: 234.00
The average of the 2 th student: 78.00

The 3 student got fail mark

The total marks of 3 th student: 69.00
The average of the 3 th student: 23.00
--*/

61. Program to retrieve the mailing address using structures

```c
/*Retrieve the address using door no*/
#include<stdio.h>
#include<conio.h>

struct address
{
char name[20];
int d_no;
char addr[30];
long int p_code;
}home[3];

void main()
{
int i,num=0;
clrscr();
printf("Enter the Home Address\n\n");
printf("Name Door_ No Street_Name Pin\n\n");
for(i=0;i<3;i++)
{
scanf("%s %d %s %ld",home[i].name,&home[i].d_no,home[i].addr,&home[i].p_code);
}
while(num!=9999)
{
printf("\n\nEnter the door no to retrive the address:\t");
scanf("%d",&num);
for(i=0;i<3;i++)
{
if(num==home[i].d_no)
break;
}
```

```c
if(i==3)
printf("\nThe door number does not exist");
else
printf("\n\nName: %s \nDoor No: %d \nStreet Name: %s \nPin: %ld",home[i].name,home[i].d_no,home[i].addr,home[i].p_code);
}
getch();
}
```

```
/*--------------------------------------------------
Output:
Enter the Home Addresses
Name Door_No Street_Name Pin
Kannan 12 North_Street 621010
Mani   23 South_Street 621011
Samy   34 Wext_Street 621012

Enter the door no to retrieve the address:    23
Name: Mani
Door_No: 23
Street_Name: South_Street
Pin: 621011

Enter the door no to retrieve the address:    9999
The door no does not exist
---------------------------------------------------*/
```

62. Program to calculate the sum of all the elements in a matrix

```c
/* Program to calculate the sum of all the elements in a matrix */
#include<stdio.h>
#include<conio.h>
void main()
{
int a[10][10],i,j,m,n,sum=0;
clrscr();
printf("Enter the order of the matrix: ");
scanf("%d %d",&m,&n);
```

```
printf("Enter the elements of the matrix: ");
for(i=0;i<m;i++)
for(j=0;j<n;j++)
scanf("%d",&a[i][j]);
for(i=0;i<m;i++)
for(j=0;j<n;j++)
sum=sum+a[i][j];
printf("Sum of elements of the matrix: %d",sum);
getch();
}
```

```
/* ------------------------------------
Output:
Enter the order of the matrix: 3 3
Enter the elements of the matrix:
1 2 3
4 5 6
7 8 9
Sum of elements of the matrix: 45
----------------------------------------- */
```

63. Program to find whether the given is Diagonal Matrix or not

```
/* Program to find the given matrix is Diagonal Matrix */
#include<stdio.h>
#include<conio.h>
void main()
{
int a[10][10],i,j,m,n,count;
clrscr();
printf("Enter the order of the matrix: ");
scanf("%d %d",&m,&n);
printf("Enter the elements of the matrix: ");

for(i=0;i<m;i++)
for(j=0;j<n;j++)
scanf("%d",&a[i][j]);
```

```c
count=0;
for(i=0;i<m;i++)
for(j=0;j<n;j++)
{
if(((i!=j)&&(a[i][j]==0))||((i==j)&&(a[i][j]!=0)))
++count;
else
break;
}
if(count==(m*n))
printf("The given matrix is diagonal matrix\n");
else
printf("The given matrix is not diagonal matrix");
getch();
}
```

```
/*--------------------------------------------------
Output:
Enter the order of the matrix: 3 3
Enter the elements of the matrix:
1 2 3
4 5 6
7 8 9
The given matrix is not diagonal matrix

Enter the order of the matrix: 3 3
Enter the elements of the matrix:
1 0 0
0 4 0
0 0 8
The given matrix is diagonal matrix
-------------------------------------------------- */
```

64. Program to find whether the given matrix is Unit Matrix or not

```c
/* Program to find the given matrix is Unit Matrix */
#include<stdio.h>
#include<conio.h>
```

```c
void main()
{
int a[10][10],i,j,m,n,count;
clrscr();
printf("Enter the order of the matrix: ");
scanf("%d %d",&m,&n);
printf("Enter the elements of the matrix: ");
for(i=0;i<m;i++)
for(j=0;j<n;j++)
scanf("%d",&a[i][j]);
count=0;
for(i=0;i<m;i++)
for(j=0;j<n;j++)
{
if(((i!=j)&&(a[i][j]==0))||((i==j)&&(a[i][j]==1)))
++count;
else
break;
}
if(count==(m*n))
printf("The given matrix is Unit Matrix\n");
else
printf("The given matrix is not Unit Matrix");
getch();
}


/*-------------------------------------------
Output:
Enter the order of the matrix: 3 3
Enter the elements of the matrix:
1 0 0
0 1 0
0 0 1
The given matrix is Unit Matrix

Enter the order of the matrix: 3 3
Enter the elements of the matrix:
1 5 8
```

0 1 9
0 0 1
The given matrix is not Unit Matrix
-- */

65. Program to extract the diagonal elements from the given matrix

```
/* Program to extract the diagonal elements from the given matrix */
#include<stdio.h>
#include<conio.h>
void main()
{
int a[10][10],i,j,m,n,count;
clrscr();
printf("Enter the order of the matrix: ");
scanf("%d %d",&m,&n);
printf("Enter the elements of the matrix: ");
for(i=0;i<m;i++)
for(j=0;j<n;j++)
scanf("%d",&a[i][j]);
printf("The diagonal elements are: ");
for(i=0;i<m;i++)
for(j=0;j<n;j++)
{
if(i==j)
printf("%d ",a[i][j]);
}
getch();}
```

/*--
Output:
Enter the order of the matrix: 3 3
Enter the elements of the matrix:
1 2 3
4 5 6
7 8 9
The diagonal elements are: 1 5 9
---*/

66. Program to perform addition and subtraction of two matrix

```c
/* Program to perform addition and subtraction of two matrix */
#include<stdio.h>
#include<conio.h>
void main()
{
int a[10][10],b[10][10],c[10][10],d[10][10],i,j,m,n;
clrscr();
printf("Enter the order of the matrix:");
scanf("%d %d",&m,&n);
printf("Enter the first matrix elements:\n");
for(i=0;i<m;i++)
{
for(j=0;j<n;j++)
scanf("%d",&a[i][j]);
}
printf("Enter the second matrix elemets:\n");
for(i=0;i<m;i++)
{
for(j=0;j<n;j++)
scanf("%d",&b[i][j]);
}
for(i=0;i<m;i++)
{
for(j=0;j<n;j++)
{
c[i][j]=a[i][j]+b[i][j];
d[i][j]=a[i][j]-b[i][j];
}
}
printf("The addition of two matrix:\n");
for(i=0;i<m;i++)
{
for(j=0;j<n;j++)
{
printf("%d  ",c[i][j]);
}
```

```c
printf("\n");
}
printf("The Subtraction of two matrix:\n");
for(i=0;i<m;i++)
{
for(j=0;j<n;j++)
{
printf("%d  ",d[i][j]);
}
printf("\n");
}
getch();
}
```

```
/*------------------------------------------
Output:
Enter the order of the matrix: 3 3
Enter the first matrix elements:
1 1 1
1 1 1
1 1 1
Enter the second matrix elemets:
1 1 1
1 1 1
1 1 1
The addition of two matrix:
2 2 2
2 2 2
2 2 2
The Subtraction of two matrix:
0 0 0
0 0 0
0 0 0
----------------------------------------------*/
```

67. Program to perform multiplication of two matrix

```c
/* Matrix Multiplication */
#include<stdio.h>
#include<conio.h>
void main()
{
int a[10][10],b[10][10],c[10][10],i,j,k,m,n;
clrscr();
printf("Enter the order of the matrix:\n");
scanf("%d %d",&m,&n);
printf("Enter the elements of matrix1:\n");
for(i=0;i<m;i++)
{
for(j=0;j<n;j++)
{
scanf("%d",&a[i][j]);
}
}
printf("Enter the elements of matrix2:\n");
for(i=0;i<m;i++)
{
for(j=0;j<n;j++)
{
scanf("%d",&b[i][j]);
}
}
for(i=0;i<m;i++)
{
for(j=0;j<n;j++)
{
c[i][j]=0;
for(k=0;k<n;k++)
{
c[i][j] = c[i][j] + a[i][k] * b[k][j];
}
}
}
```

```c
printf("The multiplied matrix:\n");
for(i=0;i<m;i++)
{
for(j=0;j<n;j++)
{
printf("%d ",c[i][j]);
}
printf("\n");
}
getch();
}
```

```
/*--------------------------------------------
Output
Enter the order of the matrix:
3 3
Enter the elements of matrix1:
1 1 1
2 2 2
3 3 3
Enter the elements of matrix2:
1 2 3
4 5 6
7 8 9
The multiplied matrix:
12 15 18
24 30 36
36 45 54
--------------------------------*/
```

68. Program to interchange the main diagonal elements with that of the secondary diagonal elements

```c
/* Interchange the main diagonal elements with that of the secondary
diagonal elements */
#include <stdio.h>
#include<conio.h>
void main ()
```

```c
{
static int ma[10][10];
int i,j,m,n,a;
clrscr();
printf ("Enetr the order of the matix \n");
scanf ("%d %d",&m,&n);
if (m ==n )
{
printf ("Enter the co-efficients of the matrix\n");
for (i=0;i<m;++i)
{
for (j=0;j<n;++j)
{
scanf ("%dx%d",&ma[i][j]);
}
}
printf ("The given matrix is \n");
for (i=0;i<m;++i)
{
for (j=0;j<n;++j)
{
printf (" %d",ma[i][j]);
}
printf ("\n");
}
for (i=0;i<m;++i)
{
a = ma[i][i];
ma[i][i]   = ma[i][m-i-1];
ma[i][m-i-1] = a;
}
printf ("The matrix after changing the \n");
printf ("main diagonal & secondary diagonal\n");
for (i=0;i<m;++i)
{
for (j=0;j<n;++j)
{
printf (" %d",ma[i][j]);
```

}
printf ("\n");
}
}
else
printf ("The givan order is not square matrix\n");
getch();
}

/*--
Output
Enetr the order of the matix
3 3
Enter the co-efficients of the matrix
1 2 3
4 5 6
7 8 9
The given matrix is
 1 2 3
 4 5 6
 7 8 9
The matrix after changing the
main diagonal & secondary diagonal
 3 2 1
 4 5 6
 9 8 7
---*/

69. Program to find the transpose of given matrix

```
/*Transpose of matrix */
#include <stdio.h>
#include<conio.h>
void main ()
{
static int mat[10][10];
int i,j,m,n;
clrscr();
```

```c
printf ("Enter the order of the matrix \n");
scanf ("%d %d",&m,&n);
printf ("Enter the elements of the matrix\n");
for (i=0;i<m;++i)
{
for (j=0;j<n;++j)
{
scanf ("%d",&mat[i][j]);
}
}
printf ("Transpose of the given matrix is \n");
for (j=0;j<n;++j)
{
for (i=0;i<m;++i)
{
printf (" %d",mat[i][j]);
}
printf ("\n");
}
getch();
}
```

/*--
Output:
Enter the order of the matrix
3 3
Enter the elements of the matrix
1 2 3
4 5 6
7 8 9
Transpose of the given matrix is
1 4 7
2 5 8
3 6 9
---*/

70. Program to extract the lower diagonal elements from the given matrix

```
/* Extract the lower diagonal elements from the given matrix */
#include<stdio.h>
#include<conio.h>
void main()
{
int a[10][10],i,j,m,n;
clrscr();
printf("Enter the order of the matrix: ");
scanf("%d %d",&m,&n);
printf("Enter the elements of the matrix: ");
for(i=0;i<m;i++)
for(j=0;j<n;j++)
scanf("%d",&a[i][j]);
printf("The lower diagonal elements are: ");
for(i=0;i<m;i++)
for(j=0;j<n;j++)
{
if(i==j)
break;
else
printf("%d ",a[i][j]);
}
getch();
}

/*--------------------------------------------
Output:
Enter the order of the matrix: 3 3
Enter the elements of the matrix:
1 2 3
4 5 6
7 8 9
The lower diagonal elements are: 4 7 8
------------------------------------------------- */
```

71. Program to compare two strings

```c
/* Comparison of strings */
#include<stdio.h>
#include<conio.h>
void main()
{
char str1[15],str2[15];
int i;
clrscr();
printf("Enter two strings U want to compare:\n");
scanf("%s %s",str1,str2);
i=0;
while(str1[i]==str2[i]&&str1[i]!='\0'&&str2[i]!='\0')
i=i+1;
if(str1[i]=='\0'&&str2[i]=='\0')
printf("\nResult: The strings are same\n");
else
printf("Result: The strings are not same\n");
getch();
}
```

```
/*------------------------------------------------
Output:
Enter two strings U want to compare:
kannan
kannan
Result: The strings are same

Enter two strings U want to compare:
mani
kannan
Result: The strings are not same
-------------------------------------------------*/
```

72. Program to concatenate two strings

```c
/* Concatenation of strings */
#include<stdio.h>
#include<conio.h>
void main()
{
int i,j,k;
char first_name[10],second_name[10],third_name[10];
char name[35];
clrscr();
printf("Enter three strings U want to concatenate:\n");
scanf("%s %s %s",first_name,second_name,third_name);
for(i=0;first_name[i]!='\0';i++)
name[i]=first_name[i];
name[i]=' ';
for(j=0;second_name[j]!='\0';j++)
name[i+j+1]=second_name[j];
name[i+j+1]=' ';
for(k=0;third_name[k]!='\0';k++)
name[i+j+k+2]=third_name[k];
name[i+j+k+2]='\0';
printf("\nThe Concatenated String: %s",name);
getch();
}

/*----------------------------------------------------------
Output:
Enter three strings U want to concatenate:
Vishwa
natha
Iyyar
The Concatenated String: Vishwa natha Iyyar
----------------------------------------------------------*/
```

73. Program to copy the strings and calculate the length of the string

```
/* Copying of strings & Calculation of string length */
#include<stdio.h>
#include<conio.h>
void main()
{
char string1[20],string2[20];
int i;
clrscr();
printf("Enter a string:\n");
scanf("%s",string2);
for(i=0;string2[i]!='\0';i++)
string1[i]=string2[i];
string1[i]='\0';
printf("\n");
printf("The source string: %s\n",string2);
printf("The copied string: %s\n",string1);
printf("Number of character: %d\n",i);
getch();
}

/*---------------------------------------
Output:
Enter a string:
venkatesh
The source string: venkatesh
The copied string: venkatesh
Number of character: 9
------------------------------------------*/
```

74. Program to check the palindrome string

```
/* Program to check whether it is a palindrome or not */
#include <stdio.h>
#include <conio.h>
#include <string.h>
void main()
```

```c
{
char string[25], revString[25]={'\0'};
int  i,length = 0, flag = 0;
clrscr();
fflush(stdin);
printf("Enter a string\n");
gets(string);
for (i=0; string[i] != '\0'; i++) /*keep going through each */
{
length++;
}
for (i=length-1; i >= 0 ; i--)
{
revString[length-i-1] = string[i];
}
for (i=0; i < length ; i++)
{
if (revString[i] == string[i])
flag = 1;
else
flag = 0;
}
if (flag == 1)
printf ("%s is a palindrome\n", string);
else
printf("%s is not a palindrome\n", string);
getch();
}

/*--------------------------------------------------
Output:
Enter a string
madam
madam is a palindrome
-------------------------------------------------------*/
```

75. Program to concatenate two strings using strcat() function

```c
/* String concatenation using strcat() function */
#include<stdio.h>
#include<conio.h>
void main()
{
char string1[15],string2[5];
clrscr();
printf("Enter the string:\n");
gets(string1);
printf("Enter another string:\n");
gets(string2);
strcat(string1,string2);
printf("The Concatenated String:\n");
puts(string1);
getch();
}


/*-----------------------------
Output:
Enter the string:
Dinesh
Enter another string:
kumar
The Concatenated String:
DineshKumar
--------------------------------*/
```

76. Program to compare two strings using strcmp() function

```c
/* Comparison of strings using strcmp() function */
#include<stdio.h>
#include<conio.h>
void main()
{
int x;
char string1[15],string2[15];
```

```c
clrscr();
printf("Enter the strings u want to compare:\n");
scanf("%s %s",string1,string2);
x=strcmp(string1,string2);
if(x==0)
printf("\nResult: The strings are same");
else
printf("\nResult: The strings are not same");
getch();
}

/*--------------------------------------
Output:
Enter the strings u want to compare:
kannan
kannan
Result: The strings are same

Enter the strings u want to compare:
james
jesus
Result: The strings are not same
----------------------------------------*/
```

77. Program to copy two strings using strcpy() function

```c
/* Copying of strings using strcpy() function */
#include<stdio.h>
#include<conio.h>
void main()
{
char string1[15],string2[5];
clrscr();
printf("Enter a String:\n");
scanf("%s",string2);
strcpy(string1,string2);
printf("The source string: %s\n",string2);
printf("The copied string: %s",string1);
```

getch();
}

/*---------------------------------
Output:
Enter a String:
Santhosh
The source string:
Santhosh
The copied string:
Santhosh
-----------------------------------*/

78. Program to reverse the given string using strrev() function

```
/* Reversing of strings using strrev() function */
#include<stdio.h>
#include<conio.h>
void main()
{
char a[20];
clrscr();
printf("Enter the string:\n");
gets(a);
printf("The reversed string: %s",strrev(a));
getch();
}
```

/*---------------------------------
Output:
Enter the string:
kannan
The reversed string:
nannak
-----------------------------------*/

79. Program to convert the case of the strings to upper case

```
/* Convert the case of the strings to upper case */
#include<stdio.h>
#include<conio.h>
void main()
{
char a[20];
clrscr();
printf("Enter the string:\n");
gets(a);
printf("The case changed string: %s",strupr(a));
getch();
}
```

```
/*-----------------------------------------
Output:
Enter the string:
kannan
The case changed string: KANNAN
---------------------------------------------*/
```

80. Program to find sum of series (1+2+3+....+n)

```
/* Sum of series (1+2+3+....+n)*/
#include<stdio.h>
#include<conio.h>
void main()
{
int n;
float series;
clrscr();
printf("Enter the limit:\n");
scanf("%d",&n);
series=(n*(n+1))/2;
printf("The sum of series(1+2+3....+n):\n%f",series);
getch();
}
```

```
/*----------------------------------------
Output:
Enter the limit:
10
The sum of series(1+2+3+....+10):
55.000000
------------------------------------------*/
```

81. Program to find the sum of series (1^3+2^3+3^3+....+n^3)

```
/* Sum of series (1^3+2^3+3^3+....+n^3)*/
#include<stdio.h>
#include<conio.h>
void main()
{
int n;
float series;
clrscr();
printf("Enter the limit:\n");
scanf("%d",&n);
series=(n*n*(n+1)*(n+1))/4;
printf("The sum of series(1^3+2^3+3^3+....+n^3):\n%f",series);
getch();
}
```

```
/*----------------------------------------------------
Output:
Enter the limit:
5
The sumo of series(1^3+2^3+3^3+....+n^3):
225.000000
------------------------------------------------------*/
```

82. Program to calculate the sum of 1/n series

```
/* Sum of 1/n series*/
#include<stdio.h>
#include<conio.h>
```

```c
void main()
{
float sum;
int n,lim;
clrscr();
sum=0;
printf("Enter the limits:\n");
scanf("%d",&lim);
for(n=1;n<=lim;++n)
{
sum=sum+1/(float)n;
printf("%2d %6.4f\n",n,sum);
}
getch();
}


/*-----------------------------------
Output:
Enter the limits:
5
 1 1.0000
 2 1.5000
 3 1.8333
 4 2.0833
 5 2.2833
--------------------------------------*/
```

83. Program to find the sum of cos(x) series

```c
/* Cos(x) series*/
#include <stdio.h>
#include <conio.h>
#include <math.h>
#include <stdlib.h>
void main()
{
int  n, x1;
float  acc, term, den, x, cosx=0, cosval;
```

```c
clrscr();
printf("Enter the value of x (in degrees)\n");
scanf("%f",&x);
x1 = x;
x = x*(3.142/180.0);   /* Converting degrees to radians*/
cosval = cos(x);
printf("Enter the accuary for the result\n");
scanf("%f", &acc);
term = 1;
cosx = term;
n = 1;
do{
den = 2*n*(2*n-1);
term = -term * x * x / den;
cosx = cosx + term;
n = n + 1;
}
while(acc <= fabs(cosval - cosx));
printf("Sum of the cosine series     = %f\n", cosx);
printf("Using Library function cos(%d) = %f\n", x1,cos(x));
getch();
}


/*------------------------------------------------
Output:
Enter the value of x (in degrees)
30
Enter the accuary for the result
0.000001
Sum of the cosine series     = 0.865991
Using Library function cos(30) = 0.865991
-------------------------------------------------*/
```

84. Program to sort the given marks using pointers

```c
/*Sorting using pointers*/
#include<stdio.h>
#include<conio.h>
```

```c
void sort(int m,int *x);
void main()
{
int i,n;
int marks[25];
clrscr();
printf("Enter the limit: ");
scanf("%d",&n);
printf("Enter the marks: ");
for(i=0;i<n;i++)
scanf("%d",&marks[i]);
sort(n,marks);
printf("The marks after sorting: ");
for(i=0;i<n;i++)
printf("%d ",marks[i]);
getch();
}

void sort(int m,int *x)
{
int i,j,temp;
for(i=1;i<=m-1;i++)
for(j=1;j<=m-1;j++)
if(*(x+j-1)>=*(x+j))
{
temp= *(x+j-1);
*(x+j-1)= *(x+j);
*(x+j)=temp;
}
}

/*-----------------------------------
Output:
Enter the limit: 3
Enter the marks: 2 1 3
The marks after sorting: 1 2 3
---------------------------------------*/
```

85. Program to find largest number using pointers

```c
/*Program to find largest number*/
#include<stdio.h>
#include<conio.h>
int *larger(int *,int *);
void main()
{
int a=25,b=35;
int *p;
clrscr();
printf("The given number is 25 & 35\n");
p=larger(&a,&b);
printf("The largest number is: %d",*p);
getch();
}

int *larger(int *x,int *y)
{
if(*x>*y)
return(x);
else
return(y);
}

/*----------------------------------
Output:
The given number is 25 and 35
The largest number is: 35
-------------------------------------*/
```

86. Program to swap two numbers using pointers

```c
/* Program to swap two numbers using pointers */
#include<stdio.h>
#include<conio.h>
void exchange(int *,int *);
void main()
```

```c
{
int x,y;
clrscr();
x=100;
y=200;
printf("Before exchange : x = %d y = %d\n\n",x,y);
exchange(&x,&y);
printf("After exchange : x = %d y = %d\n\n",x,y);
getch();
}

void exchange(int *a,int *b)
{
int t;
t=*a;
*a=*b;
*b=t;
}


/*----------------------------------------
Output:
Before exchange : x = 100 y = 200
After exchange : x=200 y = 100
------------------------------------------*/
```

87. Program to find the sum of squares of N numbers

```c
/*Program to find sum of squares of N numbers*/
#include<stdio.h>
#include<conio.h>
int sum(int (*)(int),int);
int square(int);
void main()
{
int num;
clrscr();
printf("Enter the limit:");
scanf("%d",&num);
```

```c
printf("The sum of squares of first %d numbers is
%d",num,sum(square,num));
getch();
}

int sum(int (*fptr)(),int n)
{
int add,i;
for(i=1;i<=n;i++)
add+=(*fptr)(i);
return 0;
}

int square(int i)
{
return(i*i);
}
```

```
/*-------------------------------------------------
Output:
Enter the limit: 5
The sum of squares of first 5 numbers is 55
---------------------------------------------------*/
```

88. Program to find length of the string using pointers

```c
/*Program to find length of the string*/
#include<stdio.h>
#include<conio.h>
void main()
{
char *name;
int length;
char *cptr = name;
clrscr();
printf("Enter your string: ");
gets(name);
while(*cptr != '\0')
```

```c
{
cptr++;
}
length=cptr - name;
printf("\nLength of the string = %d\n",length);
getch();
}
```

/*-----------------------------------
Output:
Enter your string: kannan
Length of the string = 6
------------------------------------*/

89. Program to count the number of vowels using pointers

```c
/* Count the number of vowels */
#include<stdio.h>
#include<conio.h>
void scan_line(char line[],int *pvow);
void main()
{
char line[80];
int vowels=0;
clrscr();
printf("Enter a line of text:\n");
scanf("%[^\n]",line);

scan_line(line,&vowels);
printf("\nNumber of Vowels:  %d",vowels);
getch();
}

void scan_line(char line[],int *pvow)
{
char ch;
int count=0;
while((ch=toupper(line[count]))!='\0')
```

```
{
if(ch=='A'||ch=='E'||ch=='I'||ch=='O'||ch=='U')
++ *pvow;
++count;
}
return;
}
```

```
/*--------------------------------------------------
Output:
Enter a line of text:
Venkatesh
Number of Vowels: 3
----------------------------------------------*/
```

90. Program to find the cube of a given number using macro definition

```
/* Cube of a given number using macro definition */
#include<stdio.h>
#include<conio.h>
#define CUBE(x) (x*x*x)
void main()
{
int x;
float y;
clrscr();
printf("Enter the value:\n");
scanf("%d",&x);
y=CUBE(x);
printf("The cube of given value: %f",y);
getch();}
```

```
/*-------------------------------------------
Output:
Enter the value:
3
The cube of given value: 27.000000
----------------------------------------------*/
```

91. Program to find the area of circle using macro definition

```c
/* Area of circle using macro definition */
#include<stdio.h>
#include<conio.h>
#define AREA(R) (2*3.14*R)
void main()
{
int x;
float y;
clrscr();
printf("Enter the radius of circle:\n");
scanf("%d",&x);
y=AREA(x);
printf("The area of the circle: %f",y);
getch();
}

/*----------------------------------------
Output:
Enter the radius of circle:
10
The area of the circle: 62.799999
-----------------------------------------*/
```

92. Program to demonstrate the nesting of macros

```c
/* Nesting of Macros */
#include<stdio.h>
#include<conio.h>
#define SQUARE(x) ((x)*(x))
#define CUBE(x) (SQUARE(x)*(x))
void main()
{
int num,squ,cub;
clrscr();
printf("Enter a number:\n");
scanf("%d",&num);
```

```
squ=SQUARE(num);
cub=CUBE(num);
printf("The Square:  %d\n",squ);
printf("The Cube  :  %d",cub);
getch();
}


/*-----------------------------------
Output:
Enter a number:
3
The Square:  9
The Cube  :  27
-----------------------------------*/
```

93. Program to illustrate the usage of #ifdef, #ifndef

```
/* Illustration of preprocessor */
#include<stdio.h>
#include<conio.h>
#define MAX 100
void main()
{
clrscr();
#ifdef MAX
printf("The MAX is defined\n");
#else
printf("The MAX is not defined\n");
#endif

#ifndef MIN
printf("The MIN is not defined\n");
#endif

#undef MAX
#ifdef MAX
printf("The MAX is defined\n");
#else
```

```
printf("The MAX is not defined\n");
#endif
getch();
}
```

```
/*-----------------------------
Output:
The MAX is defined
The MIN is not defined
The MAX is not defined
------------------------------*/
```

94. Program to illustrate the usage of Token Pasting Operator

```
/* Illustration of preprocessor */
#include<stdio.h>
#include<conio.h>
#define join(a,b) a##b
void main()
{
int cd = 100;
clrscr();
printf("%d",join(c,d));
getch();
}
```

```
/*---------------
Output:
100
----------------*/
```

95. Program to perform queue operations

```
/*Queue implementation using arrays */
#include<stdio.h>
#include<conio.h>
#define MAX 3
```

```c
struct queue
{
int ele[MAX];
int front;
int rear;
}q;

void main()
{
int choice, num, i;
clrscr();
q.front=0;
q.rear=-1;
printf("Queue Operations\n");
printf("1. Insert \n2. Delete \n3. Empty Check\n");
printf("4. Display\n5. Exit\n");
do
{
printf("\nEnter your choice:\t");
scanf("%d",&choice);
switch(choice)
{
case 1:
if(q.front > q.rear)
{
q.front = 0;
q.rear = -1;
}
printf("Enter the number to insert:\t");
scanf("%d",&num);
if(q.rear==MAX-1)
printf("The Queue overflow occured\n");
else
q.ele[++q.rear] = num;
break;

case 2:
if(q.front > q.rear)
```

```
printf("The Queue underflow occured\n");
else
printf("The removed element is: %d",q.ele[q.front++]);
break;

case 3:
if(q.front > q.rear)
printf("The Queue is empty\n");
else
printf("The Queue is not empty\n");
break;

case 4:
for(i=q.front;i<=q.rear;i++)
printf("%d-->",q.ele[i]);
break;

case 5:
exit(0);

default:
printf("Enter the correct choice...!\n");
break;
}
}
while(choice != 5);
getch();
}

/*-------------------------------------------
Output:
Queue Operations
1. Insert
2. Delete
3. Empty Check
4. Display
5. Exit
Enter your choice:   1
```

```
Enter the number to insert: 22
Enter your choice:   1
Enter the number to insert: 33
Enter your choice:   1
Enter the number to insert: 44
Enter your choice:   4
22-->33-->44-->
Enter your choice:   1
The Queue overflow occured
Enter your choice:   2
The removed element is: 22
Enter your choice:   3
The queue is not empty
Enter your choice:   4
33-->44-->
Enter your choice:   5
-----------------------------------------*/
```

96. Program to perform stack operations

```c
/*Stack implementation using arrays*/
#include<stdio.h>
#include<conio.h>
#define MAX 3

struct stack
{
int top;
int ele[MAX];
}s;

void main()
{
int choice, x, i;
s.top=-1;
clrscr();
printf("Stack Operations\n");
printf("1. Insert(Push) \n2. Delete(Pop) \n3. Empty Check\n");
```

```c
printf("4. Display\n5. Exit\n");
do
{
printf("\nEnter the choice:\t");
scanf("%d",&choice);
switch(choice)
{
case 1:
printf("\nEnter the number to insert:\t");
scanf("%d",&x);
if(s.top==MAX-1)
printf("\nThe Stack overflow occured");
else
s.ele[++s.top]=x;
break;

case 2:
if(s.top==-1)
printf("\nThe stack underflow occured");
else
printf("\nThe deleted element: %d",s.ele[s.top--]);
break;

case 3:
if(s.top==-1)
printf("\nThe Stack is empty");
else
printf("\nThe Stack is not empty");
break;

case 4:
for(i=s.top;i>=0;i--)
printf("%d-->",s.ele[i]);
break;

case 5:
exit(0);
}
```

```
}while(choice != 5);
getch();
}
```

```
/*------------------------------------------
Output:
Stack Operations
1. Insert(Push)
2. Delete(Pop)
3. Empty Check
4. Display
5. Exit
Enter your choice:  1
Enter the number to insert: 22
Enter your choice:  1
Enter the number to insert: 33
Enter your choice:  1
Enter the number to insert: 44
Enter your choice:  4
22-->33-->44-->
Enter your choice:  1
The Stack overflow occured
Enter your choice:  2
The removed element is: 44
Enter your choice:  3
The Stack is not empty
Enter your choice:  4
22-->33
Enter your choice:  5
------------------------------------------*/
```

97. Program to illustrate the dynamic memory allocation

```c
/* Ilustration of dynamic memory allocation */\
#include<stdio.h>
#include<conio.h>
#include<stdlib.h>
void main()
```

```c
{
char *input;
clrscr();
if((input = (char *)malloc(10)) == NULL)
{
printf("The memory allocation process failed\n");
exit(0);
}
strcpy(input,"VENKATESH");
printf("\nThe input size: %d",strlen(input));
printf("\nThe input contains: %s",input);

printf("\nNow Reallocation process done");
if((input = (char *)realloc(input,20)) == NULL)
{
printf("\nThe re_allocation process failed\n");
exit(0);
}
strcpy(input,"VENKATESH_PRABHU");
printf("\nNow, The input size: %d",strlen(input));
printf("\nNow, The input contains: %s",input);

free(input);
getch();
}

/*------------------------------------------
Output:
The input size: 9
The input contains: VENKATESH
Now Reallocation process done
Now, The input size: 15
Now, The input contains: VENKATESH_PRABHU
---------------------------------------------*/
```

98. Program to read and write characters in file

```
/* Simple FILE concept */
#include<stdio.h>
#include<conio.h>
void main()
{
FILE *f1;
char ch;
clrscr();
printf("The input data:\n");
f1 = fopen("INPUT","w");
while((ch=getchar()) != EOF)
putc(c,f1);
fclose(f1);
printf("\nThe output data:\n");

f1 = fopen("INPUT","r");
while((ch=getc(f1)) != EOF)
printf("%c",ch);
fclose(f1);
getch();
}


/*-------------------------------------------------------------
Output:
The input data:
This is simple file concept in C programming^z
The output data:
This is simple file concept in C programming
---------------------------------------------------------------*/
```

99. Program to separate positive and negative numbers using files

```
/*Separation of positive and negative numbers using files */
#include<stdio.h>
#include<conio.h>
void main()
```

```c
{
FILE *f1,*f2,*f3;
int number,i;
clrscr();
printf("Contents of SOURCE file\n\n");
f1 = fopen("SOURCE", "w");
for(i = 1; i <= 30; i++)
{
scanf("%d",&number);
if(number == 9999)
break;
putw(number,f1);
}
fclose(f1);
f1 = fopen("SOURCE","r");
f2 = fopen("POSITIVE","w");
f3 = fopen("NEGATIVE","w");
while((number = getw(f1)) != EOF)
{
if(number > 0)
putw(number, f2);
else
putw(number,f3);
}
fclose(f1);
fclose(f2);
fclose(f3);

f2 = fopen("POSITIVE","r");
f3 = fopen("NEGATIVE","r");

printf("\nContents of POSITIVE file\n");
while((number=getw(f2)) != EOF)
printf("%4d",number);
printf("\n\nContents of NEGATIVE file\n");
while((number=getw(f3)) != EOF)
printf("%4d",number);
```

```
fclose(f2);
fclose(f3);

getch();
}
```

```
/*-----------------------------------------
Output:
Contents of SOURCE file
12 23 -34 45 -56 -67 78 -89 9999
Contents of POSITIVE file
12 23 45 78
Contents of NEGATIVE file
-34 -56 -67 -89
-----------------------------------------*/
```

100. Program to calculate the total marks using files

```
/*Usage of fscanf & fprintf*/
#include<stdio.h>
#include<conio.h>

void main()
{
FILE *fptr;
int mark1,mark2,mark3,total,i;
clrscr();
fptr=fopen("MARK","w");
printf("Mark1 Mark2 Mark3\n\n");
for(i=1;i<=3;i++)
{
fscanf(stdin, "%d %d %d", &mark1,&mark2,&mark3);
fprintf(fptr, "%d %d %d", mark1,mark2,mark3);
}
fclose(fptr);
fprintf(stdout, "\n\n");
fptr=fopen("MARK","r");
for(i=1;i<=3;i++)
```

```
{
total=0;
fscanf(fptr, "%d %d %d", &mark1,&mark2,&mark3);
total=mark1+mark2+mark3;
fprintf(stdout, "The total: %d\n",total);
}
fclose(fptr);
getch();
}


/*--------------------------------
Output:
Mark1 Mark2 Mark3
10 10 10
20 20 20
30 30 30
The total: 30
The total: 60
The total: 90
--------------------------------*/
```

Part - II

ANSI C SYNTAX RULES

01. Documentation Statements

Syntax:
    /*...*/   - Multi line comment line
    //   - Single line comment line

Example:
    /* Program to add two numbers and
       subtract two numbers */
    //addition statement

02. Link Statements

Syntax:
    #include<header_file_name>

Example:
    #include<stdio.h>
    #include<conio.h>

03. Main Function

Syntax:
```
main()
{
Declaration statements;
Execution statements;
}
```

Example:
```
main()
{
int a,b,c;     //declaration statement
....
....
c=a+b;//execution statement
}
```

04. Variable Declaration

Syntax:
    data_type var1, var2,...,varN;
Example:
    int a;
    float a,b,c;
    char ch;

(Note: The variable name
- must start with an alphabet;
- must consist of only letters, digits and underscore;
- length should be within 31 characters;
- cannot use keywords, white spaces;)

05. Variable Initialization

Syntax:
    data_type var1;
    var1 = value;
Example:
    int a;
    a = 10;

06. Variable Declaration & Initialization

Syntax:
    data_type var1 = value;
Example:
    float b = 10.5;
    int a = 10, c = 3;

07. Typedef Declaration

Syntax:
    typedef data_type identifier;
Example:
    typedef int age;

typedef float salary;

08. Enumerated Declaration

Syntax:
> enum identifier {var1, var2, var3,....,varN};

Example:
> enum month {Jan, Feb,....,Dec};
> enum week {Mon=1, Tue,...,Sat};

09. Constant Declaration

Syntax:
> const data_type var_name = value;

Example:
> const int count = 100;
> const float max = 100.00;

10. Volatile Declaration

Syntax:
> volatile data_type var_name;

Example:
> volatile int month;

11. Storage Class Declaration

Syntax:
> auto data_type var_name;
> static data_type var_name;
> extern data_type var_name;
> register data_type var_name;

Example:
> auto int count;
> static float mark;
> extern int age;
> register float salary;

12. Symbolic Constant Definition

Syntax:
>#define identifier const_value

Example
>#define MAX 100
>#define PI 3.14

13. Expression Statement

Syntax:
>var_name = expression;

Example:
>a = b + c;
>d = d/(n+1);

14. Arithmetic Operators

+ , - , * , / , %

Example:
>c = a + b;
>d = a % b;

15. Relational Operators

< , <= , > , >= , == , !=

Example:
>if(a>b)
>{...}
>while(a!=0)
>{...}

16. Logical Operators

&& , || , !

Example:
>a>b && b<c
>a!=0 || b>c

17. Increment, Decrement Operators

++ , --

Example:
   a++;   //postfix increment operator
   b--;   //postfix decrement operator
   ++c;   //prefix increment operator

18. Conditional Operator

Syntax:
   exp1 ? exp2 : exp3;
Example:
   c = a>b ? a : b;

19. Bitwise Operator

& , | , ^ , << , >>

Example:
   b = a >> 2;
   c = a & b;

20. Sizeof Operator

Syntax:
   var_name = sizeof(var);
Example:
   int total;
   x = sizeof(total);

21. Type Conversion

Syntax:
   Var_name = (data_type)expression;
Example:
   int x;
   x = (int)4.8 + (int)2.6;   //float into int conversion

22. Short Hand Assignment

Syntax:
    var_name op = exp;   // op – operator; exp – expression

Example:
    a += 1;   //a = a+1;
    b /= 5;   //b = b/5;

23. Reading Character

Syntax:
    char var_name = getchar();

Example:
    char city = getchar();

24. Reading a String

Syntax:
    char var_name[20];
    gets(var_name);

Example:
    char name[10];
    gets(name);

25. Writing a Character

Syntax:
    putchar(var_name);

Example:
    char ch = 'Z';
    putchar(ch);

26. Writing a String

Syntax:
    puts(var_name);

Example:
    char name[10];

gets(name);
puts(name);

27. Scanf Statement

Syntax:
    scanf("control_string", &var1, &var2,...,&varN)

Example:
    scanf("%d %d", &a, &b);
    scanf("%d %f %c %s", &a, &b, &c, name);

28. Printf Statement

Syntax:
    printf("control string",var1, var2,...,varN);

Example:
    printf("%d %d",a, b);
    printf("%d %f %c", a, b, c);

29. Simple if Statement

Syntax:
```
if(test_condition)
  {
    block1_statements;
  }
```

Example:
```
if(a>b)
  {
    printf("A is greater");
  }
```

30. If-else Statement

Syntax:
```
if(test_condition)
  {
    block1_statements;
```

```
            }
        else
        {
            block2_statements;
        }
```
Example:
```
        if(a>b)
        {
            printf("A is greater");
        }
        else
        {
            printf("B is greater");
        }
```

31. Nested if-else Statement

Syntax:
```
        if(test_condition1)
        {
            if(test_condition2)
                { block1_statements; }
            else
                { block2_statements; }
        }
        else
        {
            block3_statements;
        }
```
Example:
```
        if(a>b)
        {
            if(a>c)
            printf("A");
            else
            printf("C");
        }
        else
```

```
    {
        printf("B");
    }
```

32. If-else Ladder Statement

Syntax:
```
        if(test_contidition1)
            block1_statement;
        else if(test_condition2)
            block2_statement
        else if(test_condition3)
            block3_statement;
        else
            default statement;
```
Example:
```
    if(a==1)
        printf("One");
    else if(a==2)
        printf("Two");
    else if(a==3)
        printf("Three");
    else
        printf("Not Integer");
```

33. Switch Statement

Syntax:
```
        switch(test_condition)
        {
        case val_1:
            block1_statement;
            break;
        case val_2:
            block2_ statement;
            break;
        ...
        ...
```

```
            default:
                default_block_statement;
                break;
        }
Example:
        switch(choice)
        {
        case 1:
            printf("One");
            break;
        case 2:
            printf("Two");
            break;
        ....
        ....
        default:
            printf("Not Number");
            break;
        }
```

34. Goto Statement

Syntax:
```
        Forward jump:
        goto label;
        ....
        ....
        Label:
        block_statement;

        Backward jump:
        label:
        block_statement;
        ....
        ....
        goto label;
```
Example:
```
        Forward jump:
```

```
        goto read;
        ....
        ....
        read:
        printf("Read_statment");

        Backward jump:
        read:
        printf("Read_statement");
        ....
        ....
        goto read;
```

35. While Loop Statement

Syntax:
```
        while(test_condition)           //Entry controlled loop
        {
        block_statements;
        }
```
Example:
```
        int a = 0;
        while(a<10)
           {  printf("%d",a);
              a++;
           }
```

36. Do-While Loop Statement

Syntax:
```
        do      //Exit controlled loop
          {
           block_statements;
        }
        while(test_condition);
```
Example:
```
        int a=0;
        do
```

```
        {
            printf("%d",a);
            a++
        }while(a<10);
```

37. For Loop Statement

Syntax:
```
        for(initialization; test_condition; increment)
        {
            block_statements;
        }
```
Example:
```
        for(int i=0; i<10; i++)
        {
            printf("%d",i);
        }
```

38. Array Declaration

Syntax:

One dimensional array:
    data_type array_name[size];

Two dimensional array:
    data_type array_name[size1][size2];

Multi dimensional array:
    data_type array_name[size1] [size2].... [sizeN]

Example:
```
        Int a[10];              //one dimensional
        Float b[10][10];        //two dimensional
        Double c[10][10][10];   //three dimensional
```

39. Array Initialization

Syntax:

One dimensional array:
data_type array_name[size] ={val1, val2,...,valN};
Two dimensional array:

```
data_type array_name[size1][size2] ={ {val1_1,val1_2,...val1_N},
{val2_1,val2_2,...val2_N}...};
```
Example:
```
int marks[3] = {10, 20, 30};
char john[4] = {'J','O','H','N'};
int num[2][3] = {{1, 2, 3}, {4, 5, 6}};
```

40. Function Declaration

Syntax:
```
funct_return_type funct_name( parameter_list );
```
Example:
```
int addition ( int a, int b);
float division(float, float);
```

41. Function Definition

Syntax:
```
funct_return_type funct_name (parameter_list)
{
variable declaration;
excutable statements;
....
....
return statement;
}
```
Example:
```
int addition( int a, int b)
{
int c;        //declaration
c = a + b;    //addition
return (c);   //return statement
}
```

42. Function Call

Syntax:
```
var_name = funct_name(parameter_values);
```

Example:
>   d = addition(10, 20);
>   e = division(15.5, 5.5);

43. Structure Definition

Syntax:
>   struct tag_name
>   {
>   data_type element1;
>   data_type element2;
>   .....
>   .....
>   };

Example:
>   struct student
>   {
>   int roll_no;
>   char name[10];
>   };

44. Structure Variable Declaration

Syntax:
>   struct tag_name var1, var2, var3;

Example:
>   struct student
>   {
>   int roll_no;
>   char name[10];
>   };
>   struct student stu_1, stu_2, stu_3;

45. Structure Definition and Declaration

Syntax:
>   struct tag_name
>   {

```
        data_type element1;
        data_type element2;
        }var1, var2, var3;
Example:
        struct student
        {
        int roll_no;
        char name[10];
        }stu_1, stu_2, stu_3;
```

46. Structure Initialization

Syntax:
```
        struct tag_name var1 = {element_values};
```

Example:
```
        struct student
        {
        int mark1;
        int mark2;
        };
        struct student stu_1 = {89, 90};
```

47. Union Definition and Declaration

Syntax:
```
        union tag_name
        {
        data_type element1;
        data_type element2;
        ...
        ...
        }var1, var2;
```
Example:
```
        union book_bank
        {
        char author[15];
```

float prize;
int pages;
}book1, book2;

48. Union Initialization

Syntax:
> union tag_name var1 = {element_values};

Example:
> union book_bank book1 = { "venkatesh", 100.00, 130 };

49. Bit Field Declaration

Syntax:
> struct tag_name
> {
> data_type element1: bit_length;
> data_type element2: bit_length;
> data_type element3: bit_length;
> }var1;

Example:
> struct port_status
> {
> unsigned cts: 1;
> unsigned dsr: 1;
> unsigned ring: 1;
> }status;

50. Pointer Declaration

Syntax:
> data_type *var_name;

Example:
> int *n;
> float *m;

51. Pointer Initialization

Syntax:
> ptr_var = &var_name;

Example:
> int *n;
> int m;
> n = &m;   //initialization

52. Pointer Declaration and Initialization

Syntax:
> data_type *ptr_var = &var_name;

Example:
> int m;
> int *n = &m;

53. Chain of Pointers

Syntax:
> data_type **ptr_var;

Example:
> int x;
> int *ptr1;
> int **ptr2;
> ptr1 = &x;
> ptr2 = &ptr1;

54. Function Pointer Declaration

Syntax:
> data_type(*funct_ptr)();

Example:
> int add (int, int);
> int (*ptr1)();   //declaration
> ptr1=add;   //initialization
> (*ptr1)(a,b);   //function call using pointer

55. Macro Definition

Syntax:
   #define identifier expression

Example:
   #define MAX 100
   #define CUBE(x) ((x) * (x) * (x))
      #define MAX(a,b) ((a>b)?(a):(b))

56. Preprocessor #if #else Statement

Syntax:
   #if condition
   true_statement;
   #else
   false_statement;
   #endif

Example:
   #if MAX > 99
   printf("Greater");
   #else
   printf("Smaller");
   #endif

57. Preprocessor #ifdef, #ifndef Statement

Syntax:
   #ifdef sym_const
   true_statement;
   #endif
   #undef sym_const;
   #ifndef sym_const
   true_statement;
   #else
   false_statement;
   #endif

Example:
```
#define MAX 100
#ifdef MAX
printf("MAX defined");
#endif
#undef MAX;
#ifdef MAX
printf("MAX defined");
#else
printf("MAX is not defined");
#endif
```

Part - III

ANSI C LIBRAY FUNCTIONS

ANSI C Programming Guide

01. CHARACTER FUNCTIONS

isalnum(ch)	Determine whether the argument is alphanumeric. Return a nonzero value if true; 0 otherwise.
isalpha(ch)	Determine whether the argument is alphabet. Return a nonzero value if true; 0 otherwise.
isascii(ch)	Determine whether the argument is ASCII character. Return a nonzero value if true; 0 otherwise.
iscntrl(ch)	Determine whether the argument is control character. Return a nonzero value if true; 0 otherwise.
isdigit(ch)	Determine whether the argument is decimal digit. Return a nonzero value if true; 0 otherwise.
isgraph(ch)	Determine whether the argument is graphic printable character. Return a nonzero value if true; 0 otherwise.
islower(ch)	Determine whether the argument is lower case letter. Return a nonzero value if true; 0 otherwise.
isodigit(ch)	Determine whether the argument is octal digit. Return a nonzero value if true; 0 otherwise.
isprint(ch)	Determine whether the argument is printable character. Return a nonzero value if true; 0 otherwise.
ispunct(ch)	Determine whether the argument is punctuation character. Return a nonzero value if true; 0 otherwise.
isspace(ch)	Determine whether the argument is space, horizontal tab, vertical tab, formfeed, carriage return or new line character. Return a nonzero value if true; 0 otherwise.
isupper(ch)	Determine whether the argument is upper case letter. Return a nonzero value if true; 0 otherwise.

isxdigit(ch)	Determine whether the argument is hexadecimal digit. Return a nonzero value if true; 0 otherwise.
toascii(ch)	Convert the argument to ASCII.
tolower(ch)	Convert the argument to lowercase letter.
toupper(ch)	Convert the argument to uppercase letter.

02. STRING FUNCTIONS

strcat(s1,s2)	Concatenates the two strings s1, s2.
strcmp(s1,s2)	Compares the two strings s1, s2.
strcpy(s1,s2)	Copies the contents of s2 to s1.
strlen(s1)	Finds the length of string s1.
strrev(s1)	Reverse the string s1.
strlwr(s1)	Converts the string s1 to lowercase.
strupr(s1)	Converts the string s1 to uppercase.
strcmpi(s1,s2)	Compares the two strings s1, s2 with out case sensitive.
strdup(s1)	Duplicates the string s1.
strncpy(s1,s2,n)	Copies first n characters of string S2 into S1.
strncmp(s1,s2,n)	Compares first n characters of two strings.
strncat(s1,s2,n)	Concatenates first n characters of string s2 into s1.
strstr(s1,s2)	Finds first occurrence of a string s2 in the string s1.
strchr(s1,ch)	Finds first occurrence of character ch in the string s1.
strrchr(s1,ch)	Finds last occurrence of character ch in the string s1.

03. MATHEMATICAL FUNCTIONS

acos(arg)	Returns the arc cosine of arg.
asin(arg)	Returns the arc sine of arg.
atan(arg)	Returns the arc tangent of arg.
atan2(x,y)	Returns the arc tangent of x/y.
ceil(arg)	Returns the smallest integer not less than arg.
cos(arg)	Returns the cosine of arg.
cosh(arg)	Returns the hyperbolic cosine of arg.
exp(arg)	Returns the natural logarithm base e raised to the arg power.
floor(arg)	Returns the largest integer not greater than arg.
fabs(arg)	Returns the absolute value of arg.
fmod(x,y)	Returns the remainder of x/y.
log(arg)	Returns the natural logarithm for arg.
log10(arg)	Returns the base 10 logarithm for arg.
pow(x,y)	Returns x raised to the y power.
sin(arg)	Returns the sine of arg.
sinh(arg)	Returns the hyperbolic sine of arg.
sqrt(arg)	Returns the square root of arg.
tan(arg)	Returns the tangent of arg.
tanh(arg)	Returns the hyperbolic tangent of arg.

04. DYNAMIC ALLOCATION FUNCTIONS

malloc(size)	Allocates size bytes of memory from heap.
calloc(num, size)	Allocates memory the size of num * size.
realloc(ptr, size)	Reallocates the previously allocated memory.
free(ptr)	Free a block of allocated memory indicated by ptr.

05. UTILITY FUNCTIONS

abort()	Causes abnormal termination of program.
abs(num)	Returns absolute value of num.
atof(str)	Converts the string to a double precision quantity.
atoi(str)	Converts the string to an integer.
atol(str)	Converts the string to a long interger.
div(n,d)	Returns the numerator and denominator of the division.
exit()	Causes normal termination of program.
rand()	Generates sequence of random numbers.
srand(n)	Used to set the starting point for the random numbers generated by rand() function.

06. INPUT/OUTPUT FUNCTIONS

getchar()	Reads a character from keyboard.
putchar()	Writes a character on screen.
gets()	Reads a string from keyboard.
puts()	Writes a string on screen.
getch()	Reads a character without echo.

scanf()	Reads all built-in data types from keyboard.
printf()	Writes all built-in data types on screen.
fopen()	Opens a file.
fclose()	Closes a file.
putc()	Writes a character to a file.
fputc()	Writes a character to a file.
getc()	Reads a character from a file.
fgetc()	Reads a character from a file.
fgets()	Reads a string from a file.
fputs()	Writes a string to a file.
fseek()	Seeks to a specified byte in a file.
ftell()	Returns current file position.
fprintf()	printf() statement for file.
fscanf()	scanf() statement for file.
feof()	Returns true if end of file is reached.
ferror()	Returns true if error had occurred.
rewind()	Resets the file position indicator to the beginning of the file.
remove()	Erases a file.
fflush()	Flushes a file.

Part - IV

ANSI C REFERENCES

01. HEADER FILES

alloc.h	Memory management funtions.
assert.h	Assertion macros.
bcd.h	BCD math functions.
bios.h	Bios functions like inpotrb, outportb, etc.
complex.h	Math functions for complex numbers.
conio.h	MS-DOS Console IO Functions.
constrea.h	Defines the class constream, which writes output to the screen.
ctype.h	Character conversion macros and functions.
dir.h	Directory and path information struct, macros and functions.
direct.h	POSIX directory functions.
dos.h	MS-DOS and 8086 specific functions.
errno.h	Error code definitions.
fcntl.h	Defines constants used in library function open.
float.h	Functions realted to floating-point number.
fstream.h	Declares classes that support file input and output.
generic.h	Contains macros for generic class declarations.
graphics.h	Contains all graphics related functions.
io.h	Contains structures and declarations for low-level input/output routines.
iomanip.h	Declares the C streams I/O manipulators.
iostream.h	Declares the basic C streams (I/O) routines.
limits.h	Contains environmental parameters and compile-time limitations.
locale.h	Declares language-specific information.

malloc.h	Memory management functions.
math.h	Declares prototypes for the math functions.
mem.h	Declares the memory-manipulation functions.
memory.h	Memory manipulation functions.
new.h	Access to operator new and newhandler.
process.h	Contains declarations for the spawn and exec functions.
search.h	Declares functions for searching and sorting.
setjmp.h	Defines a type used by longjmp and setjmp.
share.h	Defines parameters used in functions that use file-sharing.
signal.h	Defines constants and declarations for signal and raise.
stat.h	Returns information for the stat, fstat, lstat, statx, and fstatx subroutines.
stdarg.h	Used to parse the variable number of arguments.
stddef.h	Defines several common data types and macros.
stdio.h	Defines types and macros needed for the Standard I/O rountines and stream-level I/O routines.
stdiostr.h	Declares the C stream classes for use with stdio FILE structures.
stdlib.h	Standard library functions including conversion and search/sort routines.
string.h	Declares several string and memory manipulation routines.
strstrea.h	Declares the C stream classes for use with byte arrays in memory.
time.h	Defines a structure filled in by the time-conversion routines.

02. TYPE CONVERSION CHARACTERS

%c	Single character
%d	Decimal integer
%e	Floating point value (scientific notation)
%f	Floating point value (decimal notation)
%g	Floating point value
%h	Short integers
%i	Signed decimal, hexadecimal or octal integer
%o	Octal integers
%s	String of characters
%p	Pointer
%u	Unsigned decimal integers
%x	Hexadecimal integers
%%	Prints % sign
%[ ]	Set of characters

03. KEY WORDS

auto	extern	sizeof
break	float	static
case	for	struct
char	goto	switch
const	if	typedef
continue	int	union
default	long	unsigned
do	register	void

double	return	volatile
else	short	while
enum	signed	

04. ESCAPE SEQUENCES

\a	Single character
\b	Decimal integer
\t	Floating point value (scientific notation)
\n	Floating point value (decimal notation)
\v	Floating point value
\f	Short integers
\r	Signed decimal, hexadecimal or octal integer
\"	Octal integers
\'	String of characters
\?	Pointer
\\	Unsigned decimal integers
\0	Hexadecimal integers
\N	Prints % sign
\xN	Set of characters

05. DATA TYPES

char	8 bits
unsigned char	8 bits
signed char	8 bits
int	16 or 32 bits

unsigned int	16 or 32 bits
signed int	16 or 32 bits
short int	16 bits
unsigned short int	16 bits
signed short int	16 bits
long int	32 bits
signed long int	32 bits
unsigned long int	32 bits
float	32 bits
double	64 bits
long double	80 bits

06. PRE-PROCESSORS

#define	Defines preprocessor macros.
#error	Defines compilation error.
#include	Defines inclusive of preprocessor files.
#elif	Defines conditional inclutions.
#if	Defines conditional inclutions.
#line	Defines line number.
#else	Defines conditional inclutions.
#ifdef	Defines conditional inclutions.
#pragma	Defines diverse options to the compiler.
#endif	Defines conditional inclutions.
#ifndef	Defines conditional inclutions.
#undef	Un-defines preprocessor macros.

Part - V

ANSI C APTITUDE QUESTIONS

C APTITUDE QUESTIONS

01. ```
    main()
    {
    int *p,*q;
    p=(int *)1000;
    q=(int *)2000;
    printf("%d",(q-p));
    }
    ```
    Answer:
    500

02. ```
    main()
    {
    char *p = "hello world!";
    p[0] = 'H';
    printf("%s",p);
    }
    ```
    Answer:
    Hello world

03. ```
    main()
    {
    int a=10,b=20;
    a>=5?b=100:b=200;
    printf("%d\n",b);
    }
    ```
    Answer:
    Error

04. ```
    main()
    {
    char s[ ]="man";
    int i;
    for(i=0;s[ i ];i++)
    printf("\n%c%c%c%c",
           s[ i ],*(s+i),*(i+s),i[s]);
    }
    ```
    Answer:
    mmmm
    aaaa
    nnnn

05. ```
    main()
    {
    printf("%c",7["sundaram"]);
    }
    ```
    Answer:
    m

06. ```
    struct x
    {
    int i;
    char c;
    }
    union y
    {
    struct x a;
    double d;
    };
    main()
    {
    printf("%d",sizeof(union y));
    }
    ```
    Answer:
    8

07. ```
    main()
    {
    static int var = 5;
    printf("%d ",var--);
    if(var)
        main();
    }
    ```
    Answer:
    5 4 3 2 1
    ```

08. ```
main()
{
    int c[ ]={2.8,3.4,4,6.7,5};
    int j,*p=c,*q=c;
    for(j=0;j<5;j++) {
        printf(" %d ",*c);
        ++q; }
    for(j=0;j<5;j++){
        printf(" %d ",*p);
        ++p; }}
```
**Answer:**
2 2 2 2 2 2 3 4 6 5

09. ```
main()
{
    int i=-1,j=-1,k=0,l=2,m;
    m=i++&&j++&&k++||l++;
    printf("%d %d %d %d %d",
            i,j,k,l,m);
}
```
Answer:
0 0 1 3 1

10. ```
main()
{
    char *p;
    printf("%d %d ",
        sizeof(*p),sizeof(p));
}
```
**Answer:**
1 2

11. ```
main()
{
    int q=2,d=3,st;
    st=q*d/4-12/12+12/3*16/d;
    printf("st=%d",st);
}
```
Answer:
21

12. ```
#define int char
main()
{
    int i=65;
    printf("sizeof(i)=%d",
            sizeof(i));
}
```
**Answer:**
sizeof(i)=1

13. ```
main()
{
    printf("\nab");
    printf("\bsi");
    printf("\rha");
}
```
Answer:
hai

14. ```
#define square(x) x*x
main()
{
    int i;
    i = 64/square(4);
    printf("%d",i);
}
```
**Answer:**
64

15. ```
main()
{
    int i=5;
    printf("%d%d%d%d%d%d",
        i++,i--,++i,--i,i);
}
```

Answer:
    45545

16. ```
    #include <stdio.h>
    #define a 10
    main()
    {
    #define a 50
    printf("%d",a);
    }
    ```
    Answer:
        50

17. ```
    #define clrscr() 100
    main()
    {
    clrscr();
    printf("%d\n",clrscr());
    }
    ```
    Answer:
        100

18. ```
    #define inc(x) x++
    main()
    {
    int t=1;
    printf("%d",inc(t++));//error
    }
    ```
    Answer:
        Compiler error

19. ```
    main()
    {
    char *p="Venkatesh";
    *++p;
    printf("%s",p)
    *++p;
    printf("%s",*p)
    ```
    }
    Answer:
        enkatesh nkatesh

20. ```
    main()
    {
    printf("%p",main);
    }
    ```
    Answer:
        Some address printed.

21. ```
    main()
    {
    int i=400,j=300;
    printf("%d..%d");
    }
    ```
    Answer:
        400..300

22. ```
    main()
    {
    int i=5;
    i=!i>3;
    printf("%d",i);
    }
    ```
    Answer:
        0

23. ```
    main()
    {
    int a[10];
    3[a]=10;
    printf("%d",*(a+3));
    }
    ```
    Answer:
        10

24. ```
main()
{
int i;
printf("%d",scanf("%d",&i));
// value 10 is given as input here
}
```
**Answer:**
    1

25. ```
#define f(g,g2) g##g2
main()
{
int var12=100;
printf("%d",f(var,12));}
```
Answer:
    100

26. ```
main()
{
extern var;
printf("%d", var);
}
int var=100;
```
**Answer:**
    100

27. ```
main()
{
int i=-1;
+i;
printf("i = %d, +i = %d \n",i,+i);
}
```
Answer:
    i = -1, +i = -1

28. ```
main()
{
char *str1="abcd";
char str2[]="abcd";
printf("%d %d %d",sizeof(str1),
        sizeof(str2),sizeof("abcd"));
}
```
**Answer:**
    2 5 5

29. ```
main()
{
int *ptr;
{int i=10;
ptr=&i;}
printf("%d",*ptr);
}
```
Answer:
    10

30. ```
main()
{
int i=-1;
-i;
printf("i = %d, -i = %d \n",i,-i);
}
```
**Answer:**
    i = -1, -i = 1

31. ```
main()
{
int i=5,j=6,z;
printf("%d",i+++j);
}
```
Answer:
    11

32. main()
    {
    printf("%u",main);
    }
    Answer:
    657 (Some address value)

33. main()
    {
    char S[6]=" HELLO";
    printf("%s ",S[6]);
    }
    Answer:
    (null)

34. main()
    {
    int i=_1_abc(10);
    printf("%d\n",--i);
    }
    int _1_abc(int i)
    {
    return(i++);
    }
    Answer:
    9

35. main()
    {
    int i =0;j=0;
    if(i && j++)
    printf("%d..%d",i++,j);
    printf("%d..%d,i,j);
    }
    Answer:
    0..0

36. main()
    {
    int i;
    i = abc();
    printf("%d",i);
    }

    abc()
    {
    _AX = 1000;
    }
    Answer:
    1000

37. main()
    {
    int a= 0;int b = 20;
    char x =1;char y =10;
    if(a,b,x,y)
    printf("hello");
    }
    Answer:
    hello

38. main()
    {
    char *p;
    p="%d\n";
    p++;
    p++;
    printf(p-2,300);
    }
    Answer:
    300

39. main()
    {
    static int i=5;

```
        if(--i){
        main();
        printf("%d ",i);
        }
        }
```
Answer:
    0 0 0 0

40. ```
    main()
    {
    static int i=i++, j=j++, k=k++;
    printf("i = %d j = %d k = %d",
            i, j, k);
    }
    ```
    Answer:
        i = 1 j = 1 k = 1

41. ```
    main()
    {
    int a[10];
    printf("%d",*a+1-*a+3);
    }
    ```
    Answer:
        4

42. ```
    #define prod(a,b) a*b
    main()
    {
    int x=3,y=4;
    printf("%d",prod(x+2,y-1));
    }
    ```
    Answer:
        10

43. ```
    main()
    {
    int a[10];
    printf("%d",((a+9) + (a+1)));
    }
    ```
    Answer:
        Compiler error

44. ```
    main()
    {
    char nums[5][6]={"Zero","One",
        "Two","Three","Four"};
    printf("%s is %c",&nums[4][0],
                nums[0][0]);
    }
    ```
    Answer:
        Four is Z

45. ```
    int swap(int *a,int *b)
    {
    *a=*a+*b;*b=*a-*b;*a=*a-*b;
    }
    main()
    {
    int x=10,y=20;
    swap(&x,&y);
    printf("x= %d y = %d\n",x,y);
    }
    ```
    Answer:
        x = 20 y = 10

46. ```
    main()
    {
    int i=5;
    printf("%d",i=++i ==6);
    }
    ```
    Answer:
        1
    ```

47. main()
    {
    int i=5,j=10;
    i=i&=j&&10;
    printf("%d %d",i,j);
    }
    Answer:
        1 10

48. main()
    {
    int i;
    for(i=0;i<3;i++)
    {
    int i=100;
    i--;
    printf("%d..",i);
    }
    }
    Answer:
        99 99 99

49. main()
    {
    printf("%d",printf("ABC\\"));
    }
    Answer:
        ABC\4

50. main()
    {
    void swap();
    int x=10,y=8;
    swap(&x,&y);
    printf("x=%d y=%d",x,y);
    }
    void swap(int *a, int *b)
    {
    *a ^= *b, *b ^= *a, *a ^= *b;
    }
    Answer:
        x=10 y=8

51. main()
    {
    int i = 257;
    int *iPtr = &i;
    printf("%d %d", *((char*)iPtr),
                ((char)iPtr+1));
    }
    Answer:
        1 1

52. main()
    {
    int i=7;
    printf("%d",i++*i++);
    }
    Answer:
        56

53. #define one 0
    main()
    {
    #ifdef one
    printf("one is defined");
    #ifndef one
    printf("one is not defined");
    }
    Answer:
        one is defined

54. main()
    {
    char s[]={'1','2','3',0,'1','2','3'};
    printf("%s",s);

}
Answer:
　　123

55. main()
{
int s=5;
printf("%d"s,s<<2,s>>2);
}
Answer:
　　5 20 1

56. main()
{
int a[2][2]={2,3};

printf("%d%d%d%d", a[0][0],
　　a[0][1],a[1][0],a[1][1]);
}
Answer:
　　2300

57. main()
{
int i=-3,j=2,k=0,m;
m=++j&&++i&&++k;
printf("%d%d%d",i,j,k,m);
}
Answer:
　　find

58. main()
{
int k=2,j=3,p=0;
p=(k,j,k);
printf("%d\n",p);
}

Answer:
　　2

59. main()
{
int x=0,*p=0;
x++; p++;
printf ("%d and %d\n",x,p);
}
Answer:
　　1 and 2

60. main()
{
int x=10,y=15,z=16;
x=y=z;
printf("%d",x);
}
Answer:
　　16

61. main()
{
int k=10;
k<<=1;
printf("%d\n",k);
}
Answer:
　　20

62. main()
{
int i=-10;
for(;i;printf("%d\n",i++));
}
Answer:
-10 -9 -8 -7 -6 -5 -4 -3 -2 -1

63. main()
    {
    enum x {a=1,b,c,d,f=60,y}
    printf("%d",y);
    }
    Answer:
    61

64. main( )
    {
    float a = 5, b = 2 ;
    int c ;
    c = a % b ;   //error
    printf ("%d", c) ;
    }
    Answer:
    Compile time error

65. main( )
    {
    int a, b ;
    a = -3 - - 3;
    b = -3 - - (- 3) ;
    printf ("a = %d b = %d", a, b);
    }
    Answer:
    a = 0; b = - 6

66. main( )
    {
    printf ("nn \n\n nn\n") ;
    printf ("nn /n/n nn/n") ;
    }
    Answer:
    nn

    nn
    nn /n/n nn/n

67. main( )
    {
    int i ;
    for (i = 1 ; i <= 5 ;
          printf ("\n%d", i)) ;
    i++;
    }
    Answer:
    Infinite loop with printing '1'

68. main()
    {
    {#define x 10}
    printf("%d",++x);   //error
    }
    Answer:
    Compile time error

69. main()
    {
    int k = 2, j = 3, p = 0;
    p=(k, j, k);
    printf("%d",p);
    }
    Answer:
    2

70. main()
    {
    int k = 10;
    k<<=1;
    printf("%d",k);
    }
    Answer:
    20

71. main()
    {
    int i=65,j=0;
    for(;j<26; i++,j++)
    {
    printf("%s\n",i);
    }
    }
    Answer:
        Prints A to Z

72. main(int argc)
    {
    int a[] = {5,6};
    printf("%d",a[1.6]);
    }
    Answer:
        6

73. main(int argc)
    {
    int x = 1111;
    printf("%d", !x);
    }
    Answer:
    0

74. main()
    {
    printf("%d",printf("hello
            world"));
    }
    Answer:
        hello world 11

75. main()
    {
    int a[]={10,20,30,40,50};
    int *p;
    p= (int*)((char *)a + sizeof(int));
    printf("%d",*p);   }
    Answer:
        20

76. main()
    {
    int a[10]={1,2,3,4,5,6,7,8,9,10};
    int *p=a;
    int *q=&a[9];
    printf("%d",q-p+1);
    }
    Answer:
        10

77. main()
    {
    char *p1="Name";
    char *p2;
    p2=(char *)malloc(20);
    while(*p2++=*p1++);
    printf("%s\n",p2);
    }
    Answer:
        Garbage value printed

78. main()
    {
    int x=20,y=35;
    x = y++ + x++;
    y = ++y + ++x;
    printf("%d %d\n",x,y);
    }
    Answer:
        57 94

79. main()
    {
    char *ptr = "Rama Krishnan";
    (*ptr)++;
    printf("%s\n",ptr);
    ptr++;
    printf("%s\n",ptr);
    }
    Answer:
        Sama Krishnan
        ama Krishnan

80. main()
    {
    int a[] ={ 1,2,3,4,5,6,7};
    char c[] = {'a','x','h','o','k'};
    printf("%d\t %d ", (&a[3]-
        &a[0]),(&c[3]-&c[0]));
    }
    Answer:
        3   3

81. main()
    {
    int i,j;
    int mat[3][3] =
    {1,2,3,4,5,6,7,8,9};
    for (i=2;i>=0;i--)
    for (j=2;j>=0;j--)
    printf("%d" , *(*(mat+j)+i));
    }
    Answer:
        9 6 3 8 5 2 7 4 1

82. main()
    {
    int n=2;
    printf("%d %d\n", ++n, n*n);
    }
    Answer:
        3,4

83. main()
    {
    int a=10;
    int b=6;
    if(a=3)
    b++;
    printf("%d %d\n",a,b++);
    }
    Answer:
        3,7

84. main()
    {
    int i,*p=&i;
    p=malloc(10);
    free(p);
    printf("%d",p);
    }
    Answer:
        Garbage value

85. main()
    {
    int x,j,k;
    j=k=6;x=2;
    x=j*k;
    printf("%d", x);
    }
    Answer:
        36

86. ```
main()
{
    int i=20,k=0,j;
    for(j=1;j<i; j=1+4*(i/j))
    {
        k+=j<10?4:3;
    }
    printf("%d", k);
}
```
**Answer:**
    k=4

87. ```
int i =10;
main()
{
    int i =20,n;
    for(n=0;n<=i;)
    {
        int i=10;
        i++;
    }
    printf("%d", i);
}
```
Answer:
    20

88. ```
main()
{
    int y=10;
    if(y++>9 && y++!=10 &&
                y++>10)
    {
        printf("%d", y);
    else
        printf("%d", y);
}
```
**Answer:**
    13

89. ```
main()
{
    int x = 2, y=6,z=6;
    x=y==z;
    printf("%d",x);
}
```
Answer:
    1

90. ```
#define VALUE 1+2
main()
{
    printf("%d and %d\n",
    VALUE/VALUE,VALUE*3);
}
```
**Answer:**
    5 and 7

91. ```
main( )
{
    unsigned int i=3;
    while( i >=0)
        printf( "%d", i--);
}
```
Answer:
    Infinite loop

92. ```
main( )
{
    int x,y, z;
    x=2;
    y=5;
    z= x+++y;
    printf("%d %d %d", x, y z);
}
```
**Answer:**
    3 5 7
```

93. ```
    main()
    {
        int i=2;
        i++;
        if(i=4)
        {printf(i=4);}   //error
        else
        {printf(i=3);}   //error
    }
    ```
    Answer:
    Error-Type mismatch

94. ```
    main()
    {
        int i=100,j=20;
        i++=j;   //error
        i*=j;
        printf("%d\t%d\n",i,j);
    }
    ```
    Answer:
    Error

95. ```
    main()
    {
        int a[]={9,4,1,7,5};
        int *p;
        p=&a[3];
        printf("%d",p[-1]);
    }
    ```
    Answer:
    1

96. ```
    main()
    {
        int a=5;
        const int *p=&a;
        *p=200;        //error
        printf("%d",*p);
    }
    ```
    Answer:
    Compile Error

97. ```
    #define SQ(x) x*x
    main()
    {
        int a=SQ(2+1);
        printf("%d",a);
    }
    ```
    Answer:
    5

98. ```
    # define prod(a,b) a*b
    main()
    {
        int x=2;
        int y=3;
        printf("%d",prod(x+2,y-1));
    }
    ```
    Answer:
    7

99. ```
    main()
    {
        int x=5, *p;
        p=&x
        printf("%d",++*p);
    }
    ```
    Answer:
    6

100. ```
     main()
     {
         int i=1;
         i=i+2*i++;
         printf(%d,i);
     }
     ```

Answer:
    4

101. ```
#define MAX(x,y) (x)>(y)?(x):(y)
main()
{
  int i=10,j=5,k=0;
  k= MAX(i++,++j)
  printf("%d %d %d",i,j,k)
}
```
**Answer:**
    12 6 11

102. ```
main()
{
printf("hello");
fork();      //error
}
```
Answer:
    Linker Error

103. ```
main()
{
int const * p=5;
printf("%d",++(*p));   //error
}
```
**Answer:**
    Compiler error

104. ```
main()
{
extern int i;
i=20;         //error
printf("%d",i);
}
```
Answer:
    Linker Error

105. ```
#define dprint(expr)   printf(#expr   "=%d\n",expr)
main()
{
int x=7;
int y=3;
dprintf(x/y);
}
```
**Answer:**
    x/y=2

106. ```
int x= 0x65;
main()
{
char x;
printf("%d\n",x)
}
```
Answer:
    -113

107. ```
main()
{
int a=10;
int b=6;
if(a=3)
b++;
printf("%d %d\n",a,b++);
}
```
**Answer:**
    3 7

108. ```
main(int argc)
{
int a;
printf("%d",a);
}
```
Answer:
    Garbage Value

109. main()
    {
    int i=-10;
    for(;i;printf("%d\n",i++));
    }
    Answer:
        Prints -10 to -1

110. main()
    {
    int i=3,a=4,n;
    float t=4.2;
    n=a*a/i+i/2*t+2+t;
    printf("%d",n);
    }
    Answer:
        15

111. #define int char
    main()
    {
    int i=65;
    printf("sizeof(i)=%d",sizeof(i));
    }
    Answer:
        sizeof(i)=1

112. main( )
    {
    int first, last ;
    if (first == 1 & last == 0)
    printf ("\nProgramming in C") ;
    }
    Answer:
    Run. Nothing will be displayed.

113. #define max 100
    main()
    {
    #define max 200
    Printf("%d",max);
    }
    Answer:
        200

114. main()
    {
    int num1=200;
    int num2=300;
    printf("%d %d");
    }
    Answer:
        200 300

115. main( )
    {
    int m = 1, n = 2 ;
    if (m = 5) && if (n = 10) //error
    printf ("\nI'm Venkatesh") ;
    }
    Answer:
    Expression syntax error

116. #define getch() 100
    main()
    {
    printf("%d",getch());
    getch();
    }
    Answer:
        100

117. #define fun(a,b) a##b
```
main()
{
int xy=200;
printf("%d",fun(x,y));
}
```
Answer:
    200

118.
```
main()
{
display();
}
void display()
{
printf("Im Venkatesh");
}
```
Answer:
    Compiler error

119.
```
main()
{
const int num=1;
int num2;
num2 = ++num1; //error
printf("%d",num2);
}
```
Answer:
    Compiler error

120.
```
main()
{
char arr[]="abcdefg\0";
int len=strlen(arr);
printf("length=%d",++len);
}
```
Answer:
    length=8

121. # define max 100; //error
```
main()
{
printf("%d",max);
}
```
Answer:
    Compile Error

122.
```
main()
{
int i=10;
if(printf("%d\n",i))
{printf("True");}
else
{printf("False")
}
}
```
Answer:
    10
    True

123.
```
main()
{
static int num;
num=num++;
printf("%d",num);
}
```
Answer:
    1

124.
```
main()
{
char *ptr = "Venkatesh";
char ch;
ch=++*(ptr++);
printf("%c",ch);     }
```
Answer:
    W

125. main()
    {
    Int a=5,b=5;
    Printf("%d",(a==b));
    }
    Answer:
        1

126. #define ctrstr "%d\n"
    main()
    {
    int num=1;
    printf(ctrstr,num);
    }
    Answer:
        1

127. main()
    {
    register int num=20;
    printf("Address: %d",&num);
    }
    Answer:
        Compiler Error

128. main()
    {
    int i=10;
    printf("Address:%u",&i);
    printf("Value:%d",*(&i));
    }
    Answer:
        Address: 65530
        Value: 10

129. main()
    {
    int a;
    float b;
    sanf("%d %f",&b,&a);
    pintf("%d %f", a,b);
    }
    Answer:
        Compiler error

130. main()
    {
    funct(funct());
    }
    funct()
    {
    printf("Inside function");
    }
    Answer:
        Compiler error

131. main()
    {
    char chr=100;
    printf("%d",chr);
    }
    Answer:
        100

132. #define max 100
    main()
    {
    #ifndef max
    printf("True");
    #else
    printf("False");
    #endif
    }
    Answer:
        False

133. main()
{
    int case=10;   //error
    printf("%d",case);
}
Answer:
    Compiler error

135. main()
{
    int 1_num=89;   //error
    printf("%d",1_num);
}
Answer:
    Compiler error

136. main()
    char arr1[]="world";
    char arr2[]=
        {'w','o','r','l','d'};
    printf("%s s",arr1,arr2);
}
Answer:
    world world

137. main()
{
    float a;
    a = 4*5/5+5-6*6+1;
    printf("%f",a);
}
Answer:
    -26.000000

138. main()
{
    int x;
    printf("%d",x=10);
}
Answer:
    10

139. main()
    {static int a,b,c,d;
    if(a+b == c+d)
    printf("Equal");
    else
    printf("Not equal");
}
Answer:
    Equal

140. main()
{
    static int i;
    if(i=5 && i>2)
    printf("True");
    else
    printf("False");
}
Answer:
    False

141. main()
{
    float a=12.5456;
    printf("%6.2f %f",a,a);
}
Answer:
    12.54 12.545600

142. main()
{
    for(;;)
    {
    printf("printf");

}
}
Answer:
    Infinite loop

143. ```
main()
{static int i;
for(;i!=0;i++)
{printf("printf");}
printf("Loop Over");
}
```
**Answer:**
    Loop Over

144. ```
#define MAX 100
main()
{
printf("%d",max);
}
```
Answer:
    Compiler error

145. ```
const int i=10;
main()
{
int i=20;
printf("%d",i);
}
```
**Answer:**
    20

146. ```
main()
{
int num[4]={1,2};
printf("%d %d",num[2],num[3]);}
```
Answer:
    0 0

147. ```
main()
{
int x=5,y=10,z=15,a;
a=x<y<z;
printf("%d",a);
}
```
**Answer:**
    1

148. ```
main()
{
printf("Good" "Boy");
}
```
Answer:
    GoodBoy

149. ```
main()
{
int num1,num2=10;
num1 = num2+5+NULL;
printf("%d",num1);
}
```
**Answer:**
    15

150. ```
main()
{
int arr[]={1,2,3};
printf("%d  %d",arr,&arr[0]);
}
```
Answer:
    -16 -16
    (Same address value)

www.ingramcontent.com/pod-product-compliance
Lightning Source LLC
Chambersburg PA
CBHW080914170526
45158CB00008B/2101